Developing Your Child's Emotional Intelligence

Ten Steps To Self-Control From Birth to Age Three

Cover design by Wellness Institute, Inc.

SelfHelpBooks.com
A division of Wellness Institute, Inc.
Heritage Office Park
107 Whitney Avenue
Gretna, LA 70056

Wellness Institute, Inc.
Gretna, LA 70056

ISBN 1587411202

Developing Your Child's Emotional Intelligence

Ten Steps To Self-Control From Birth to Age Three

Margaret Altman M.S.

Avi Bitton, M.S.

Rebecca Reyes, M.D.

TABLE OF CONTENTS

A Message from the Authors

Our ten steps contain the 10 vital capacities that lead to *self-control*. Yes, self-control: a basic and vital human capacity. We have found that self-control is the *foundation* of emotional intelligence . These 10 steps will lead you and your child to this empowering ability.

Emotional Intelligence is an ability that has been widely discussed and it is considered to be more important than academic intelligence. That is because emotional intelligence is the amazing ability to understand and control our emotions in the face of challenges, changes and crises. One way to appreciate this ability is this; before you can use your intelligent mind to solve problems you must have some control over your fluctuating emotions, some ability to balance yourself emotionally, and use problem solving skills. This is the heart of emotional intelligence. We all know people who have this capacity. These people tend to have long term success in their work and personal relationships when others around them explode or implode. Such individuals who maintain their emotional balance look so natural when they do it. It seems to be instinctive. It is not. Emotional intelligence is a mature ability and it takes time and practice for this ability to become part of the human psyche.

We have discovered how emotional intelligence develops from the earliest age possible and from its roots in **self-control** Our 10 steps trace the development of self- control abilities; the keys to emotional intelligence.

A great deal of this development occurs in the first three years, well before your child must face the harsh realities and sweet temptations of the outside world. Yes, it happens this early. A child needs the skills of self control in order to succeed in life.

There are, of course, many factors that come into play as a child matures and learns the skills of emotional intelligence. But **self-control** is clearly the earliest and the most important. It is thus the focus of our book. Self-control is not inborn and is greatly influenced by the child's experiences with parents. We have therefore focused on how and when to teach the basic emotional lessons that will empower your child with self-control and emotional intelligence.

What is self-control? It is the young child's earliest abilities to manage the roller coaster of emotions and the behavior that goes with the ups, the downs and the emotional turn arounds These early abilities are learned and some of them are so small and simple that they are often overlooked. Each of these abilities is highlighted in a Step of it's own. When a child has mastered these 10 Steps then he or she is on the way to achieving Emotional Intelligence.

Self-control is empowering and we have to learn how to do it. That is why we have started with the earliest appearing capacities that lead to this wonderful skill before the child is 3 years of age. Just to name a few of the capacities that we will be describing are the following; finding and keeping a comfort zone, reading face expressions, sharing emotions, expressing negative emotions in healthy ways, etc. You may think that you recognize some of these capacities but we shed new light on what they mean, how they are linked with emotional intelligence and how they empower your child before that child is 3 years old!

The whole concept of youngsters who have emotions and behavior that are out of control is a very real and a scary one for many adults. More so recently with the reality of unexpected violence and bloody rampages by youngsters that appear in the news. These youngsters seem to have no control over their emotions and behavior. And they are so far from the goal of emotional intelligence. In many cases adults may have ignored some of the warning signs that we see in hindsight so very clearly. Those critical missed steps on the way to developing self-control are so obvious after the fact aren't they? It is so painfully clear that these individuals never completed the journey towards emotional intelligence. But when you try, after the fact, to put a finger on the specific reason for the explosion, it's harder than you think.

Our interest in this project comes from our work and our personal lives as parents and health practitioners. Dr. Reyes and M. Altman have worked together with individuals of all ages and their families in a large county hospital. In this particular setting we see some of the more dramatic cases in which emotional intelligence has never developed because of the missed Steps in the development of self-control   The tragic cases that we have witnessed occur not only in adolescents but in young children as well because lack of self-control abilities can lead quickly to crisis and hospitalization We see youngsters who are angry or unhappy and so out of control that they try to hurt others and themselves. They become stuck in some dark, unstable emotional domain, unable to find a way to manage the roller coaster of their feelings and their behavior

We also talk to adults who have never mastered the 10 Steps of self-control and who have never achieved emotional intelligence. And these adults "loose it" when something changes in their lives or when there is a crisis that pushes their emotional buttons. We have seen cases of explosive loss of self-control. These experiences have made us realize how crucial it is to develop the foundations of self-control as early as possible and to reinforce this skill throughout the life span.

So we share this information with you. Even if you have to go backwards through the steps with an older youngster who is in trouble, you will find this book helpful.

Please use our information as a guide and not as a ruler for measuring your child's capacities and your own. Keep in mind that children develop at individually unique rates and achieve goals at different times. As we present our *10 Steps*, don't worry if your child does not learn them as fast as you like. We are embarking on a life long process that is natural and will be as unique as your own child.

Although we are directing this book toward parents of young children, teachers and expectant parents, we believe that parents with older children and others who interact with young children can benefit from reading it.. For example, as you read the information in Step 1 you need not be an expectant mother to gain insights into the development of self control in your own child or in yourself.

Part One: Self-Control

Introduction
The Sources of Self Control

Two parents, Marla and Dan gaze at their newborn lying peacefully in the crib. This is their second child and yet the excitement, the pleasure is almost overwhelming. The infant's eyes open. "Is he looking at us?" Dan says in a hushed tone of voice. He leans over the infant and their breath intermingles. The mother coos, and the baby gurgles. Father joins in more loudly. After a moment the baby's face flushes and he gets restless. The parents look at each other, smile and stand silently as the baby relaxes.

We have just read about an exciting event. In just a brief moment we have witnessed something beyond parent-infant bonding. What these parents have done is to teach a first lesson in self-control. And this *a brain-changing experience*. This experience will shape this baby's brain in very vital areas. The most important area, the one that concerns us, is the area of self- control. This is the capacity to manage fluctuating emotions and behavior so that the amazing power can be harnessed and used in a positive fashion.

We will be following these parents around for a while, watching how and when they teach the lessons of self-control, and peeking into the minds of their kids. This will help us to understand how they learn the steps of self-control.

Marla and Dan are doing what a lot of parents do and most of it truly is brain building! We want to focus on exactly what they do every time that they add to this baby's and their toddler's capacity for self- control. This is the capacity that we're after because it will help make little Mike and Jill emotionally superior kids. That specifically means kids who can manage their own inner roller coaster emotions, and use their brains to decide what to do in behavior. This is real empowerment. It will take some doing to learn this capacity but that's what we're here for.

In the scene above our new parents reached in and did something for this baby that he couldn't do for himself. He will learn from what they did. The parent's interaction regulated this tiny infant's "out of control" or fluctuating emotions and behavior and brought him into a *comfort zone*. They helped this baby off of the roller coaster of emotions. Our first milestone in the self-control process is the establishment of this balanced state inside the baby. The awake, alert, aware state is what parent's are aiming for because this is an ideal state for the infant to learn and enjoy the rest of his or her lessons in self control.

If we could be inside of this baby's nervous system we would feel the roller coaster experience; the upwards climb into the heights of excitement then the downwards journey out of the stratosphere and finally the leveling out that is comfortable. This baby couldn't take this entire ride on his own. He simply doesn't have the ability to do it. When these parents continue to help him with the task of easing off of the roller coaster and into a comfort zone, he will learn to do it for himself. And it will take some time and effort from parent and child. This is only their first teaching task and his first self-control homework lesson.

Why is teaching and learning the basics of self-control *so* important when the baby can learn so many other things on his own? Parents are well aware these days that a lot is going on in this baby's brain. So much in fact that some parents are engaged in teaching infants as young a s four months of age how to distinguish one letter of the alphabet from another! Indeed the baby's brain is learning at an incredibly rapid rate from the very first moment of life. There is new research that documents that within the first few months of the baby's existence it is learning to master language. However, without the *skills* to control the roller coaster of feelings, this baby's ability to recite her ABC's just won't take her very far. And these are the skills of self-control. These skills ultimately lead to emotional intelligence.

When we talk about control we are not referring to anything harsh and punitive. It is simply the ability to change and to manage one's fluctuating emotion and behavior as it fits the situation. And this is a bit more complex than pushing some internal off or on feeling switch in the brain. Building this capacity is the objective of our *10 Steps.*

Teaching the infant, from birth how to manage emotions and behavior is the key to all of the other capacities that parents can teach. In our anecdote, Marla and Dan demonstrated some of the basic teaching techniques. They used their faces, their voices and their body language to stimulate the baby and then they used the same tools in a different way to relax the infant. They put him into a **comfort zone** that he will feel and remember as only infants remember this kind of pleasure. This is the true beginning of interactive teaching and communication.

Does this seem to be easy as pie so far? There are many things that will make this teaching/learning experience more challenging, even frustrating at times. One of these things is the basic fact that each infant has his or her own temperament, his or her own unique comfort zone. As different as their comfort zones are it is important for the infant to be assisted in finding one that works. And works in the sense of allowing them as soon as possible, to use their intelligent, thinking, planning minds to function. This is what parents are doing when they stimulate or relax an infant. They are guiding it to a balanced, comfortable state so that more and more learning can occur.

Many studies support the necessity of establishing an early Comfort Zone. Most of them emphasize that constant emotional stress on the human brain and especially the infant's fragile brain is destructive of the very structure of the brain. Stress-produced chemicals are not growth conducive.

Infants, even though they are dynamic little learning machines, cannot find their own Comfort Zones. They cannot regulate their fluctuating emotions or protect themselves from what is impacting their minds from outside. In a state of wildly fluctuating emotions, what child can hope to succeed in life?

There is astounding new information indicating that by the age of

3 months most infants can demonstrate that he or she is on the *right track* for developing self- control? Who knew that by 18 months a child can show you that she has mastered some of the most important skills? These milestones emerge in our earliest Steps. Now that you will know what to look for you can applaud the milestones much earlier and your baby will reap the benefits.

Does this seem like a big job for you and your child? It is certainly not easy to do when the pressure of work and finances intrudes. It is not always "instinctive" or "common sense" given the number of parents seeking help when their kids are wildly throwing temper tantrums. But consider this; often a little effort goes a long, long way. In terms of how the brain learns and remembers, scientists have found that once a learning connection is established it takes less and less effort to get the response. Good teaching and learning connections between you and your child will go a long way. Once a comfort zone is established it may take less work to guide the child there.

This is, of course, also the case when *bad* learning habits are established. When parents are not able or available to help the child find his balanced internal state a baby will inevitably find some way to deal with the problem. They have to find some way to get comfortable and survive. These types of comfort zones often become problems themselves. In our work, we see children who withdraw from excitement almost entirely and those who seem to crave wildly active emotional and behavioral states until they are exhausted. We also see the adolescents who use drugs and alcohol to find that elusive comfort zone. And we know that adults who loose control easily do some very destructive things to themselves and to others.

Again, you may be wondering how all of this relates to the issue of what is called "emotional intelligence." This is a term widely used in the literature to describe the kind of intelligence that is very different from reading, writing or sports abilities. Emotional intelligence is an outcome, a goal that we hope our ten steps lead to. The odds of reaching this goal are increased when infants and their parents work on it within the first three years.

And now, some parents are asking the question; "How does developing self-control differ from bonding or attaching with the infant and developing a loving relationship?"

Love, as we know, comes in many shapes and sizes. Loving feelings can be expressed softly, loudly, harshly, and punitively as in "tough love." Types of bonds between parent and infant vary extensively in their nature both within and between cultures. The parent-infant and parent-child relationship is a vehicle, a pipeline for the teaching and the learning of emotion and behavior control skills. We have seen infants develop these skills when bonded to a grand-parent, a caretaker, or even in a setting where there are multiple infants and several caretakers. It is important, therefore to look *beyond attachment* and beyond love and into the specific nature of what is being taught and learned.

What this Book Is and Isn't

There are also numerous books on the market that help parents with the wide range of early childhood concerns; feeding, sleeping, toilet training, discipline, calming and communicating. There are many books that aim to soothe the parents and reassure them about their "instinctive" or common sense skills in bringing up baby to be happy and successful.

In *this book* we focus upon the earliest developing capacity; the skill that really underlies all of the other abilities. The capacity for self-control (emotional and behavior control) is at the core of all later appearing abilities.

What good is learning to read books if the child cannot read and understand the vital emotional face and voice expressions on the teacher's face? These expressions are the signals that tell him what to do in school.

How successful will the athletic youngster be if he cannot harness the energy of his emotions and then get along with his peers?

Reading and understanding face and voice expressions is a foundation of self-control. These signals are incredible guides for our own feelings and actions.

This book will guide you in shaping your baby's brain in ways that give the child the skills to function in school, with people and in intimate relationships. And how you emotionally interact with your infant will, indeed, have an enormous impact.

The book is based upon research that has been done and is still being done in the fields of neurology, psychology, psychiatry, and rehabilitative medicine. These studies have looked at the developing brain in order to find out why and how we feel the things we feel and why we do the things that we do. We have used this information to help parents in their earliest interactions with their baby. In the first days, weeks and months the baby's brain is in a rapid state of growth and now we know that patterns and connections formed early are resistant to change. Although the brain has a degree of "plasticity", habits as we all know, are hard to break. It takes time and effort to make changes in life long patterns of feeling and behaving.

This is a book about growing up healthy and strong even when the odds may seem to be against it. As we go through the ten steps we focus on the ability of the brain to grow, to change and to be shaped by new experiences. In reality, broken steps can be fixed and there are many ways in which to repair emotional wounds between infant and child in a timely fashion.

Hey Mom and Dad, is it all up to you?

Although for many years doctors denied it, parents have known that their babies are born with their own individual temperaments. The inborn characteristics of your infant that affect the process of developing self control are many and varied. However, there are things in this domain that parents can look at, watch for and work with. Throughout the ten steps we pay attention to the infant's natural emotional and behavioral repertoire, his so called level of arousal or his tendency to be more or less excitable and/or irritable. This is one of the key markers that parents will attune to and then determine where the baby's comfort zone is. This is a very important place from which self-control skills are launched.

Parents also need to look into their own ways of controlling their emotions and behaviors. A parent who faces the world with chronic anxiety will probably teach certain self-control strategies to their infant without even knowing that they are doing so. Anxiety does not help in maintaining self-control. Anxious households produce anxious children according to the latest studies. This information increases the responsibility of parents and is also a growth experience for them. We deal with anxiety and parental self-control strategies in later sections of this book.

As we have mentioned, there are factors that parent's simply cannot control but even in these cases there are steps that you can take and things that you can do help your child learn the skills that he or she will need.

Out of step on the journey to Emotion and Behavior Control

In this book we will present cases from our practices that are dramatic. They illustrate a point in a very direct manner. Such is the case of Lilia.

Lilia is 13 months old. She was brought into the *Healthy Baby Clinic* for a routine appointment by her aunt, Mrs. R. Along with Lilia the aunt brought three other children that she is caring for. They are her nieces and nephews with ages ranging from 13 months to 5 years. The youngsters are playing and running around with other kids in the waiting room. Except for Lilia who is lying in the arms of her aunt, with her face turned away.

The pediatric nurse who does the preliminary exam on Lilia is having problems. She notes in the chart that the baby stiffens her body when the aunt tries to put her on the exam table. She writes that the baby screams when the nurse speaks, cries when she is touched, and seems inconsolable. The exam room is warm and bright. The nurse is gentle. Lilia's eyes are tightly closed and she is clutching at her aunt. Mrs. R apologizes for the child's behavior. She tells the nurse that Lilia just doesn't like to be around people very much. Other than this she believes the little girl is OK. She drinks her bottle, and is quiet most of the time if she's left alone.

"She's a good baby." The aunt says.

The notes in the chart read; "Possible developmental disorder?"

This is a dire diagnosis but trained clinicians can pick up problems early. With 13-month-old Lilia, however, something else may be going on.

Without knowing a great deal about Lilia's first months of life the nurse has picked up some vital data. This child is extremely uncomfortable with new people, in a strange environment. She is very much out of control in relation to her emotions and her behavior. This would be close to normal if her aunt were not sitting with her in the exam, but the fact that even closeness of her aunt doesn't give her a sense of security is a red flag.

Where is this child's growing ability to adapt and adjust to changes? Does she have a Comfort Zone? Did anyone ever pay attention and help her manage the roller coaster of her feelings? Without knowing the full early history of this little girl we can see that her skills in controlling her emotions and behavior are impaired. She has a Comfort Zone that requires that she be without stimulation. This is ZERO TOLERANCE. This doesn't bode well for her future in terms of learning to manage her feelings and behavior.

Lilia at 13 months has learned that in order to be comfortable she has to block out, avoid and fight off emotional stimulation from outside. Lilia's behavior shows us in a dramatic fashion exactly what lack of self-control skills look, sound and feel like. This poor child is not climbing the Steps at this point.

At the age of 13 months, children (see our Steps 4-6) are well on the way to developing self- control techniques. Although they cannot yet completely regulate their emotions and behavior they have established comfort zones, which allow them to begin to use their intelligent minds to get what they want and need. One important *milestone* of these steps is that the child may explore the environment around her in close proximity to the parent. The youngster of Lilia's age can slow down enough to read the emotional expressions in the parent's face and voice and then she responds to these emotional stimuli. Parents know these kids are picking up and beginning to understand emotional signals. And this along with their developing mobility and curiosity will launch them into the next phase.

A child such as Lilia, whose Comfort Zone is unreachable in most environments will be in a state of anxiety, of fright and unable to adjust. The comfort and quiet that she seeks is not something that she will easily find in this world.

The Ten Steps

Parents and caretakers don't ask for much, just the basics. You *do* want your child to settle into school, to listen to you and adults, to cooperate with others. You do want to be assured that if your child is snubbed at school, if he gets a poor grade, or if she has an unexpected problem, that your child is not going to throw a tantrum or reach for a gun and shoot another student, parent or teacher, or commit suicide.

You *can* give your child a tool bag full of emotional skills that allows him or her to use his mind, to cope, to curb frustration, to talk with others, to work out problems and go on living healthfully in the face of an emotional crisis.

Without the learned skills of self- control and without an internal Comfort Zone, one that he or she can reach and work from, a child may be more prone to develop such pathologies such as depression, hyperactivity, anger and violent behavior, even schizophrenia. There are studies that describe many different pathways that lead from early missed steps in self-control to aggression, depression and anxiety. Some of these sad journeys are identified in the book.

This book addresses some very important pathways to healthy and unhealthy behavior. Not all impulsive, violent behavior comes from the same sources or leads to the same consequences. And yet in our own practice and experiences we find that the core of many of these problems lies within the early developing system of self-control.

How to Use this Book

This book guides you, the parents and caretakers, in easy and understandable steps (we have tried to avoid or minimize scientific jargon) along with **evaluation tools** so that you can see how well you and your child are doing and simple **exercises**. Use this book as your first primer in your own journey towards emotional health as well as that of your child. The resource section is a gold mine of information and it allows parents and others to plan ahead by reviewing internet safe sites, and other excellent sources of interest.

Following our ten steps is not so much a daunting task as it might seem. We will be following Marla, Dan and their children as well as other people as they go through each step. You do not need to put on mental galoshes and wade through massive amounts of information. We've done that. You do not need to be perfect (none of us are). We have taken all the science and put it into ten easy steps that will amplify your enjoyment in being a parent, in having children, in watching them grow. You will be guided on how to teach the skills.

Each chapter explores one vital phase in the process of developing key skills. The steps correspond to major positive changes in your baby's brain that contribute to his growing emotional abilities. You will see that one step leads into the next in a very natural way as the brain and behavior develop interactively.

In addition to evaluation tools and exercises we have identified emotional **milestones** for each step. Some of them will amuse you and others will astound you. They should all be recognized and applauded because they lead to self- control. Here are your shining stars during the first three years.

Use this book as a guide to family health. These ten steps build emotional strength within both the child and the parent. A child cannot grow and become more present and aware without the parent also becoming more present and aware. This process is a two-way street. As you work to insure your kids get the best emotional foundation, you will also benefit. In creating family happiness, it is impossible to encourage depth and empathy, presence and compassion, intelligence and awareness within your child if you are not intending to become more integrated in these areas. The family is a unit and all of you grow emotionally strong and intelligent together.

Finally, please use this book as a guide to discovering how you developed the capacity for emotion and behavior control. Self-help and self-discovery go hand in hand as you read through the steps some of your basic questions may be answered. We hope that you uncover and understand the steps that led up to your health and any problems you may have with, for example, anxiety, guilt, self-esteem, impulse-control, or unstable moods.

Nobody's Perfect

What if you have an older child with problems and you are starting to feel guilty? Don't. There is hope. After all, therapists help adults all the time. This book is about building the foundation correctly so you don't need to repair the basic structure down the line. Armed with this information, you are way ahead of the game. Many parents and other caregivers are not aware of how the emotional connection between parent and infant grows and changes. Once you understand the steps, you can foster the development of consistent and sensitive interactions between you and the child and successfully communicate the information that leads to self-control and emotional intelligence. Understanding the process in its milestone development can help parents at any stage to strengthen the interaction or decrease its intensity as needed.

Therapists use our techniques in early stages of therapy to connect with clients in a trusting relationship. We guide clients to a comfort zone or they simply won't come back and do the rest of the therapeutic work! Therapists do the mirroring, get up close and personal in order to effect fast and long lasting changes in the clients. In child, adolescent and adult therapy, these abilities are used to help client's find their emotional balance and their emotional intelligence. It's not magic; it is a step-by-step process that every parent should know. Here is how it works.

Karen is 5 years old and she is an independent, curious, lively little girl. For the past few months she's been waking up at night and not really wanting to go to school. Her class has been sending cards to NYC in memory of the World Trade Center attack and all the little kids who lost their parents. Karen's mother and father have picked up on her changes in mood and motivation. They discussed what to do. Mother thinks that she will adjust on her own but father feels bad for her and he has started to give her extra time before bed so that he can read to her and play with her. The games are pretty babyish (hide and seek under the covers) but she smiles and laughs. He hasn't done this since she was 3 and while at first it felt a little silly to go back to these old routines he can see a change in her attitude. And to be completely honest, he doesn't mind this "special time" thing at all.

He's also paying a bit more attention to her school projects. She told him last night that he was "the best dad in the whole world" and he told her that he was very proud of her. The nightmares have decreased and Karen doesn't question the need to go to school anymore.

The steps in the book — from prenatal expectations to the first interactions when baby is born and the emergence of an infant's skills and temperament — show how targeted interaction and emotional communication grows, when it is strongest, and how to use it to support emotional skills at any age. And though it has its roots in prenatal steps and is most evident before age one, *this bond can be nurtured or made more flexible as long as we know what it is and how it develops.*

Every crisis, at any age, is an opportunity for change and for growth. Don't think you've blown it because your two year old is having a hissy fit, or you didn't do these steps with your six-year-old. Parental guilt is not a necessary or desirable part of developing self- control.

Parents can use techniques in the ten steps to re-teach emotional lessons. When caretakers know the milestones of self-control, they can go back, so to speak, and re-teach the abilities that are lacking. If parents of a one-year-old realize that their child is not looking at them when they talk, they will be able to focus on the face-to-face (mirroring) exercise that helps the child re-learn this skill. Parents of older children will be better positioned to deal with problems such as increased temper tantrums, school phobia, anxiety and depression.

Key Concepts

Emotions (Also known as affect and feeling): These are powerful subjective states that rely upon pathways in the brain and are trigged directly or indirectly by stimuli from outside and inside of the self. The primary emotions are identified as; sadness, happiness, anger, surprise, fear and disgust. Note; anxiety is part of the fear spectrum of emotions and shame is part of the disgust spectrum.

Emotional Stimuli: The emotionally expressive stimuli from face, voice, touch, smell that enter a child's senses and then impact the brain.

Comfort Zone: Awake, Alert and Aware. In a healthy sense this is an individually determined level of *balanced arousal*. It is often experienced as positive feelings of inner strength, well-being, and motivation. The Comfort Zone may be seen in the contented expressions and adaptive behaviors of infants and children.

Self-Control. This is the set of learned abilities that are the foundations of emotional intelligence. These abilities enable an individual as a child, to master the internal roller coaster of emotions and respond in adaptive, healthy ways. These abilities are initially learned through interaction with primary caretakers from birth to three years of age. They include the ability to get into a comfort zone, and to understand and respond to the emotional signals within and from outside. Self-control skills mature through trail and error during childhood and adolescence. They require a great deal of support and nurturance from involved adults along the way. These abilities are contained in the 10 Steps.

Emotional Intelligence: The mature ability to control emotions and behavior. This is the outcome of self- control development. It is the ability to manage emotions and direct behavior appropriately in times of stress, change, crisis and daily life situations.

Emotion milestones: Signs that indicate to the parents that they themselves, or their children, are achieving skills of self-control. The emotion milestones may be subtle but they let you know that the steps of each chapter are being accomplished. For example: An emotional milestone often overlooked in Step Five is the infant's **sharing** things of emotional significance by **pointing and gazing** at the parents. In subtle but powerful ways this ability to share is linked to self-control and emotional intelligence.

Part Two:

The 10 Steps to Self-Control

Step One: Pregnancy

The Birth of Self Control

The Infra Structure

"Hey honey, get in here and look at this"

Marla sighs heavily as she hoists her large body up from the chair. She had just settled down for a minute, hoping to save some energy for the evening. Little Jill had gone right to sleep for once and Marla was pretty tired. This pregnancy was definitely draining her strength. At six months she was gaining a bit more weight than "normal" and Dan seemed to think she was becoming lazy and fat. This pregnancy was definitely harder than the first one. Yet she was really happy about having a second child.

In the living room, Dan is watching a commercial showing slim pregnant women working out in a gym. They look beautiful. "That's what you need, babe." Dan says without looking at her

"OK I'll sign up at the gym this week." Marla says hoping that a few good aerobics classes will help her shape up quickly. Some of her pregnant friends were running several miles a day and they looked pretty good. Marla had a glorious moment in which she saw herself sprinting easily along the road to the admiring applause of Dan and her friends.

In order to appreciate the big picture of self-control we start from the beginning. The beginning is pregnancy and in this case, Marla's pregnancy with little Mike.

As we collectively heave a sigh for poor Marla we know that deep down old Dan is just trying to help his wife and the baby. He thinks that jumping around in an aerobics class will do the trick. Just being the helpful husband.

And he's partly right. Pregnancy is a vital preparatory stage for the infant's emotional and physical health. The building blocks of self-control are being put into place before the infant is born. The parents and the course of the pregnancy have a great role to play in our ten-step guide. This is *step one* for baby and for parents in the development of the vital capacity for emotion and behavior control. But aerobics? Would that add to the development of this capacity?

Exercise and nutrition are key factors in maintaining a "healthy" pregnancy. This is not news. Doctors and parents have been aware for some time that food and exercise count in the early development of the fetus. But very recent research is finally looking at the advice given to pregnant women a bit more closely. And pregnant women get advice from all over the place that influences the development of the baby's brain and nervous system. We have to sift through all of the new data to find the information that relates to the baby's development of self-control.

For example researchers who study pregnant women found that the intensity of the exercise during middle and late stage pregnancy may well have a negative impact upon placental growth. In fact, a high volume of moderate intensity, weight-bearing exercise at this time *reduces* placental growth. Not a healthy thing at all. Now they are looking more critically at the type, timing and intensity of exercise as it relates to vital aspects of fetal development.

Numerous studies tell us that the womb is not a protected environment and the developing fetus is profoundly impacted by the environmental matter that surrounds it. The environmental matter extends beyond the obvious toxins in the environment to those chemical messengers that convey the mother's emotional state. Before birth the baby's brain and nervous system is being shaped and influenced by the matter in its environment as well as by the genes in its DNA.

Research is piling up on how a pregnant woman's emotional state impacts fetal development in general. New research shows that anxiety during pregnancy can result in fetal growth restriction and other very serious problems.

So, lots of things impact the unborn baby. We have a deeper concern that lies beyond the size of the fetus, thought this is very important. *Beyond growth factors, we are very interested and concerned about the impact of emotional and chemical forces on the brain centers that support the self-control system.*

These particular brain systems have been the object of much research, still going on and very important. Scientists are careful to point out that it is not one but several interacting brain systems that are involved in the development of self-control. What they agree upon is that the prefrontal cortex area, which is maturing over the first and second years, is the part of the brain we must look at.

Here it is then. Whatever affects the prefrontal cortex may effect emotional development in our specific area of interest. The third trimester keeps popping up in the research as a vitally important time. In the third trimester of pregnancy studies show that there is a vast movement or migration of neurons in the cortex area and they have to find their appointed places in order for the system to work. The brain has to be wired correctly for systems to work as they should. A great deal of movement and connecting up is going on in the brain during pregnancy and a significant amount of this is within the centers for emotional and behavioral control.

If we could peer inside little Mike's brain at the tender pre-natal age of 5 months we would find that his nervous system already reacts to pain. Does Mike feel pain like adults do? Perhaps he doesn't but the pain mechanism in his brain is being wired in and it will play a part in self-control. Although he is deep inside his mother's body, Mike also responds to some sounds. Studies on this subject are interesting and from our perspective we are excited to find that his little developing brain is already "hearing" to some extent. We will see in Steps 2 and 3 just how vital sounds are for developing self control skills.

We can say with certainty that either directly or indirectly certain toxins, maternal illnesses, and maternal emotional states do have a significant impact during the third trimester. Some of these factors are easier to see and measure than others. For example, there have been many studies on the direct impact on the fetus' system of a toxic substance that the mother eats (such as a diet low in folic acid increasing the risk of birth defects), drinks (alcohol can depress the baby's brain and the immune system), handles (exposure to solvents has been linked to birth defects) or breathes (living near crowded freeways or within two miles of a toxic dump has been linked to Down's Syndrome and other birth defects).

Even though factors such as anxiety and depression are less measurable, they are now being seen as equally important and again, they influence development of brain and nervous system directly and indirectly. Emotions such as fear, anxiety and joy create changes in the mother's physiological system and these chemical changes may directly influence development. On the other hand a mother who is anxious or depressed may not care for herself as she should and this can indirectly effect the baby's development. A mother's ability to manage her own emotions and remain within her *Comfort Zone* is so very important.

We have learned, through scientific research that emotional stimuli are strong forces and that by changing internal chemistry or by influencing the mother's behavior, these emotions have an impact upon early brain development.

The Anxiety and Depression Connection

Pregnancy is a time of symptoms that are emotional as well as physical. The childbearing years in general are a time of high prevalence of mental illness. We cannot ignore the impact of a mothers' state of anxiety and depression upon the brain and nervous system of the unborn child.

There is scientific data to support the fact that stress during pregnancy alters serotonin levels in the fetal brain and can thereby impact the baby's emotional and behavioral responses after birth. Animal studies showed that animals who were subjected to stress in-utero had anxiety-related behaviors, were more easily alarmed by things around them, and were less prone to explore their environment. In human terms this kind of emotional and behavioral responding would not be considered "healthy" self-control by any means. The connection between stress in-utero and the basic capacity to understand and respond adaptively to the environment is clear in this research. On the human level, though direct pathways from mother's anxiety/depression and fetal brain centers have not been absolutely proven, the research is pointing in that direction.

The mother's emotional state and Step One are intimately related. *And so when should a mother become concerned about her level of anxiety or depression as it relates to her infant's abilities to control behavior and emotion?* When the feelings become uncomfortable and disrupt her ability to care for herself is one answer. And the other is that when depression or anxiety have, in the past, continued on into the postpartum period then the alarm bells should begin to ring.

The treatment for stress and depression is now under as much scrutiny as is the conditions themselves. This is due to the realization that medication also impacts the unborn child. There is great debate over when and how to treat women with medication and or therapy. Depression or mood swings or crippling anxiety when they are *severe* threaten the safety and health of the woman and unborn child are often aggressively treated with medications and therapy but when the problem is mild or moderate the woman is usually left to her own devices to try to cope and care for her health.

And so here we are with the understanding that depression and anxiety are not to be thought of as "normal" when they make a mother uncomfortable during her pregnancy. They certainly are not healthy for the emotional development of the baby. What is a mother to do when she finds herself stressed or sad over a period of time and she wants to make a change in the situation?

Fortunately, there is a lot of help in this area. According to many professionals and women who seek help, Cognitive Behavioral Therapy is a first line treatment for depressed and anxious pregnant women. CBT as it is called is a relatively fast, easy way to help change the individual's thoughts, feelings and behavior. Many self-help books have been written from this perspective and the results in terms of depression and anxiety are very good.

Evaluation Tools and Exercises

Mothers and significant others who want to do some important preparatory work on their own feelings and situations can begin with a straight forward evaluation of their *expectations* about the pregnancy and the baby to be born. Expectations are the hopes and fears that one has for the baby and these hopes and fears relate to the mother's mood and anxiety level.

Expectations may be positive ones, as in "I can tell that this baby will have his father's sense of humor" or negative ones, as in "I can feel that this baby is going to be difficult." A study on mother's earliest responses to their newborns in the hospital showed that from day one, the *expectations* that mother had built up during the pregnancy directly affected how she read her infant's behavior. This carried through the first year and shaped the infant's development.

And so, what are or were your expectations for your baby? Perhaps you want to do some work on this very area and modify the emotional environment within you.

The Expectation Evaluation

Here is your list of statements about your pregnancy. Divide them into positive and negative (you can put a + or – in front of the statement). Then circle the statements that are closest to how you really feel now if you are pregnant or felt when you were pregnant. When you have finished write down what you think are the negative (-) statements and transform them into positive ones. Example of a transformation follows this list:

- *I think that I am ready for this baby*
- *I feel that at this point in the pregnancy things are going well*
- *I am anxious about how my baby is developing because of things people tell me*
- *I wish I could change my living situation before the baby arrives*

22

- *I think this baby will have more opportunities that I had*
- *I worry about the world that this baby is being born into*
- *I think that this baby will have my anxious personality*
- *I think that this baby will be born with some pretty good strengths*
- *I feel embarrassed about being pregnant*
- *I think that being a parent will be easy for me*
- *I believe this baby will cause a strain on my marriage*
- *I think this baby will have his father's addictions*
- *I think this baby will have my sense of humor because I'm usually happy*
- *I think that something I did in the first trimester will harm my baby*
- *I think that this baby is developing normally at this point*
- *I think I will need a lot of help with being a good parent*
- *I have pleasant dreams about the baby*
- *I sometimes have bad dreams about the baby and they worry me.*

Here is an example of a transformation; *I sometimes have bad dreams about the baby and they worry me.* This is a pessimistic view (-) transformed into: *my dreams reflect some of the concerns I have because I am already an aware and concerned parent.* (+) Wow! What a difference! This is an important milestone for you.

Expectation Exercises to help you with daily transformations

1. Keep a list of positive expectations and say them daily.
2. Keep a pregnancy journal filled with positive baby-related articles, news stories and your own ideas.
3. Keep track of your nutrition and make sure you are staying as healthy as possible.
4. Do at least one positive thing for yourself daily; as simple as getting your hair cut, or doing some upper arm exercises so that you can hold that beautiful new infant.
5. Practice the exercises for face-reading later on in this book
6. Ask your doctor about any concerns that stay in your mind.

Another workable approach is to look at your general level of optimism. This differs from expectations and comes closest to defining and understanding your mood or mood changes during the days of your pregnancy.

Research shows that self help in this area even helps mothers with serious medical problems! Moms with diabetes and high blood pressure illnesses are considered high-risk for developing problems during pregnancy. Yet, it has been shown that if these women are *optimistic* during pregnancy, they tend to have fewer problems. And what is optimism?

It is our inner perspective or opinion about upcoming experiences and challenges. Our level of optimism or pessimism is based upon our prior successes or failures with similar experiences.

People tend to fall into one of two categories when a new or stressful situation comes up: some eagerly approach it as a challenge and others avoid it like the plague. Those who have a good track record and level of competence are usually optimistic about themselves and how they respond to the world around them.

Optimism can be felt, seen and heard by others — especially by the baby you're carrying.

Optimism Evaluation Tool

Answer the following questions Yes or No

1. *I usually see the glass as half full rather than half empty*
2. *I am more comfortable in routine, predictable situations*
3. *People tell me that I am a positive person*
4. *I look forward to the day when I wake up*
5. *I like to do new things.*
6. *People tell me that I act stressed out*
7. *In uncertain times I tend to expect the best*
8. *I get upset easily*
9. *I think that my future will be bright*
10. *I like compliments*
11. *I have few friends because so few people are trustworthy*
12. *I've been disappointed a lot in my life.*
13. *I think that I can change things for the better*
14. *I look forward to holidays*

Now, please add up the number of "yes" answers. A score of 8 or more means you are optimistic! If you have a score of less than 8 please do the following exercises.

Optimism Exercise 1

Keep a daily log and write down any self-critical thoughts that come into your mind. Next to each critical thought, write one description about yourself that is positive. So if you thought, "I am lazy," write next to it a positive thought, such as, "I am a great cook." This helps foster optimism and decrease pessimistic mental habits.

Optimism Exercise 2

In the morning, write a list of several activities you plan to do; they can be simple such as brush teeth, shop, call Mom, read the paper. At the end of the day, put a "C" for chore next to the tasks that you had to do for life maintenance and a "P" for pleasure next to the things that you enjoyed. After a couple of days note if you have as many items on your check list that give you pleasure as must-do tasks. Doing more chores than pleasurable things can certainly sour anyone's mood. If you are consistently doing more chores than pleasurable activities, make a list of what you like to do and integrate these activities into your life.

An important Emotional Milestone for parents: **notice that you are choosing to see the glass as half full most of the time, not half empty. You might see the gloomy side first, but at least you then choose to change your attitude.**

Not every parent is an immediate success story. Take the case of Maria, for example:

Maria just finished the exercises and she still doesn't feel good. She is 5 months pregnant with her second child and she remembers the trouble she had after the birth of her first baby. She shudders inwardly as she recalls feeling that she couldn't care for the infant, that the baby didn't like her at all and that she had to fake some kind of relationship with an infant who drained all of her energy. Maria's post-partum depression led to a hospitalization and to medication. She stopped the medication when she became pregnant again, but now she's worried about her mood.

At her next prenatal visit Maria has to make an important decision; to share her concerns with the nurse or pretend that everything's OK. When the clinic nurse asks her the general question "How are you doing?" how should she respond? Maria gives it some thought and she knows that she does want this pregnancy to be better. She wants to be with this infant after delivery. When she states how she feels and gives her history she's referred to the doctor who proceeds slowly and carefully with treatment for the depression. This involves therapy and, when her mood is still sad, it also involves a medication that is as safe as the doctor can prescribe. When she has her baby, Maria finds that she can cope better and actually looks forward to the infant's being brought to her. It's a new and lovely experience that will enable her to bring this baby into its comfort zone while she remains in her own balanced state.

Parental Stress, Triggers and Self -Control

When you as a parent are under stress it may affect your own self-control capacities and your ability to teach your child the important lessons in this area. Trying to help your child learn while you are not in your comfort zone can be frustrating for both of you.

Geraldo is a soon-to-be father and a husband. We will meet him later on. His wife Anna is pregnant and having a few "issues" that have to do with Geraldo's ways of dealing with stressful events. They have an older son (he is 10) and during his infancy Geraldo favored the "tough" approach to problems when they came up. When the baby couldn't sleep and Geraldo was tired he said "let him fall asleep on his own." If the baby broke a toy and Geraldo couldn't fix he was angry and raised his voice at the baby. When the baby became a toddler, Geraldo encouraged him not to run to Mom in tears and to "be a little man."

Anna knows that Geraldo needs to be in charge of any situation. He was raised to be "strong" and independent. To him that means that when the situation gets tense he has to leap to the helm and squelch the fire.

It hasn't been a problem because Anna is comfortable not being in charge. But she wonders about their 10 year old son and the new baby. Very soon there will be more stress in their family. A new baby means less money, less free time, less control over unexpected situations.

Anna has decided that both she and Geraldo have difficulty coping with the stress of unexpected emotional events. Geraldo is stressed out by any possibility of loosing control. When things are in an emotional turmoil, he has to get back in control as fast as possible. This is what she knows so far. She's having a problem understanding her own dynamics and wants to do some work before the second child arrives.

Therefore, another way of preparing for Step 2 *before* the baby arrives is to look at your own stress level and self-control system. A good way to do this begins with what is called your *stress level*. Stress is the term used for a high level of inner discomfort that tends to continue over a period of time. It can be triggered by *factors that are in your situation* as well as inside of you. Being under stress or feeling stressed out means that you are not in a healthy comfort zone. **You are probably more likely to experience a loss of control** when things get challenging or intense. Environments during the pregnancy are usually not ideal and some are very difficult. It is important to look at the outside as well as the inside when we think about what **triggers** your stress level to rise and to fall. Stress as we know from on-going warnings about the impact of stress on the heart, the mind and the spirit is something to try and avoid during pregnancy. Your stress level can be worked on if you know what things are really getting to you.

Stress Evaluation Questionnaire

For this exercise we will use the term stress to describe feelings of discomfort that may include annoyance, frustration, and sadness. You might also feel the physical symptoms such as stomach ache, mild head ache as indications that the event has stressed you.

Please answer yes or no

1. *Do minor problems and disappointments upset you excessively?*
2. *Do you feel pulled in different directions?*
3. *Do people tell you that you look "stressed"?*
4. *Do you have headaches, or other pains not associated with the pregnancy?*
5. *Do you feel inadequate when you face daily chores?*
6. *Are you constantly thinking of what you haven't accomplished during the day?*
7. *Do you have sleep problems not associated with the pregnancy?*
8. *Do you think about getting away from it all frequently?*
9. *Are you arguing more with significant people around you (spouse, boss co-worker)*
10. *Are you feeling tension in other people?*

If you answered yes to 5 or more questions, please do the following exercise.

The Stress Log Exercise

Begin a log. Divide a page into 4 sections: The Event (where, when and what happened) and The Feeling (emotional or physical sensation).

General Example 1.

Where	*When*	*What*	*Feeling*
Home	*AM*	*Spouse says he will be home too late for dinner*	*Sadness*
Work	*Noon*	*Co-workers go off to lunch without you*	*Frustration*
Home	*PM*	*Eating dinner alone*	*Sadness*

When you look at the Events you will see a pattern. The above chart shows that being left out or possibly rejected in any situation (home or work) leads to stress. Aloneness and rejection are important triggers wherever this person happens to find herself.

Here is an example of Anna's chart that will clarify what we mean

Where	When	What	Feeling
Home	AM	A bill is overdue	Headache & Anxiety
Home	After School	Child starts an argument	Anxiety
Home	Early evening	Dinner not ready on time	Stomach ache
Home	Later evening	Older child starts argument	Anxiety

Looking at this chart all situations are *at home*. There are similarities in *lateness* and *arguing* that set off Anna's stress. These are her **triggers**.

Understanding your triggers and the times and events that may set them off is half the battle. For a quick way to relieve the stress you can use these quick and reliable stress-busting methods that are found in self-help books, on the internet etc.

1. AM: Begin the morning with easy stretching exercises and breathing or yoga
2. PM: End the day with progressive relaxation exercises
3. Mid-day: Take a few minutes after lunch to close your eyes and deep breathe.
4. Anytime: The 'count-to-10' method. Just count slowly from 1 to ten breathing in with 1 and out with 2 and so on.
5. The 'breathe in and hold it for 10 seconds and breathe out' method
6. The 'visualization of a positive scene method.' See it, feel it and hear it.

7. The 'look at the situation in a humorous light' method
8. The 'progressive relaxation method:' clench fists, hold it then gradually relax your hands. Tighten arm muscles as much as you can and then relax them. Go on to leg, stomach and neck muscles.

All of these methods can help you to get back into your comfort zone.

Many parents benefit from taking a real hard look at what triggers their stress and loss of self control and what they generally do when that happens; the strategies that they use to settle the anxiety, reduce the anger or to feel better. These *strategies* are what you are going to teach your kids either directly or simply by them watching you perform in a stressful situation.

In Anna's case, for example, her triggers led to her strategies of trying to cover up or settle the situation without Geraldo knowing about it. She is the peace-maker in the family and because of her own history she tries to avoid Geraldo becoming upset. Anna benefited from looking at the list of triggers and strategies below to get a better handle on how she was managing her own roller coaster of feelings.

These are some very general common triggers and strategies that you may recognize.

Triggers	Strategies for feeling better
Being humiliated	*Angry retaliation*
Being rejected	*Staying by yourself*
Being out of control	*Demanding control back*
Losing something valuable	*Finding a replacement quickly*
Being frightened of the Unexpected	*Running away*
Feeling insecure about yourself	*Denying the feeling, acting secure*

We might say that Anna, when triggered by the unexpected and by conflict runs away emotionally and has been denying the feelings. Several of these triggers and strategies may look pretty familiar to you. Sometimes they work temporarily to get you back into a comfort zone. Often they lead to more stress later on and they do not lead to solving the problem. Do you want your baby to use any of these strategies?

It will help you to know your own triggers and to practice some of the more positive strategies for getting back into your Comfort Zone. The ways that you learn to get control of the roller coaster of emotions are the ways that your child will probably use as well. The simplest way for an adult to level out the emotional roller coaster is to do the **Stress Busting Exercises** whenever a trigger comes along.

The next step, when your roller coaster has leveled out a bit, is to use the healthy **strategies** that work for you. Now you can begin to use your mind and solve the real problem. We present the short list of **strategies** that many people use to get to the root of the problem.

1. Learn good problem solving skills; some people learn to develop priority lists, and research how the experts solve problems by making charts, developing data banks of information etc.
2. The available help network; Many people have a hot line list of people to ask about problems when they come up
3. Clear communication skills; Many adults find that expressing feelings accurately and listening to other's expressions does help to resolve problems.

Anna has done the work and she realizes why she is triggered by her fear of the unexpected and conflict. As a child her family moved around a lot, and her father drank a great deal. She was never sure when he would come home intoxicated, yell and scream. Now, she tends to run and hide her feelings when she faces uncertainty or conflict. This hasn't helped in her marriage because she is unhappy and unable to talk about it. And she is very aware that talking to Geraldo may not do the trick unless he is motivated to examine his self-control issues.

In any event she is prepared to become emotionally stronger and not run from her problems. Anna is looking into joining a support group. She may not change Geraldo's behavior but with a reduced stress level she is definitely doing something healthy for the new baby and her older son.

As you work on your own self-control system you prepare to teach your child how to do it. Kids, as we know, do what we do as well as what we tell them to do. Being an emotionally healthy adult is beneficial whether you have children or teach them or baby-sit for them or simply see them on weekends.

And now we present some information on other factors that can impact the baby's self-control system before birth. Some of this you may have already read about. The point here is that this information has become even more relevant now that we understand how the infant's brain develops in utero. We need all the data we can get in order to give the child the best chance of developing healthy self-control skills.

Cigarettes, Alcohol, Drugs and self-control

Would you want to share a smoke with your baby? Certainly not! But that's what happens when a mother-to-be inhales cigarette smoke. The baby smokes too. Prenatal exposure to nicotine has been shown to lead to dysregulation (a word for emotional imbalance) in neurodevelopment and can indicate higher risk for psychiatric problems. This means that smoking, and possibly even second-hand exposure, may not be good for the neural systems that support your baby's emotional health. And we are talking about the parts of the brain that your child will depend upon for self-control.

The same happens with drugs and alcohol. Many parents are aware of these risks. But are you aware of how these substances can shape the course of your infant's emotional growth? Numerous studies suggest that when mothers imbibe, infants show more negative emotions such as fussing, crying, or frowning when they are confronted with any frustrating event. Kids born from moms who drink during pregnancy, especially to excess, often are not skilled at self-control. They are deficient in their ability to accurately read inner and outer cues, to express feelings and to regulate their inner stress states.

Continuous Nausea and self-control

Certain situations for pregnant women have long been overlooked or taken for granted as normal. Nausea during pregnancy, for example, is considered to be an expected symptom and even when the situation is extreme, many women are advised to "put up with it".

The new data suggests that women who are nauseated during the middle and late stages of pregnancy have children with signs of poor emotional development. The children tend more toward hyperactivity and less perseverance, especially at five years of age.

This is food for thought. The researchers in this study state that it has to do with changes in the mother's blood chemistry, increased levels of urea nitrogen and ketones etc. Whatever the underlying reason for the nausea, be it anxiety or a physical problem, it needs to be addressed.

There are numerous ways to reduce nausea when it is not caused by a chronic physical condition. Please ask your doctor or nurse about the many kinds of safe treatment for nausea.

Other Serious Issues

There are some situations that can cause more stress, and therefore less opportunity for the development of healthy brain systems in the baby. The following problems may require intensive inner work by the caregiver-to-be, but if a parent's own emotional development has been hampered, the baby may suffer the consequences. It is well worth the time and effort to explore these issues.

Abuse and Victimization

An often-overlooked factor that may impact the brain of the developing fetus comes from the mother's earlier life. Many women have had traumas in their lives long before becoming pregnant.

Diane was a 26 year old woman who had to spend her entire pregnancy in a psychiatric hospital. When she was admitted, her parents said that she had a history of depression from when she was a teenager. The parents didn't give much information and appeared almost embarrassed by Diane's pregnancy and her problems.

Unfortunately Diane was too sad and too psychotic to give the staff a great deal of background. Except for one thing. She denied that she was pregnant until after she delivered the baby. She also was terrified of male staff and became aggressive when approached by her male doctor. The treatment team responsible for Diana's care worked hard with the parents to get them to share more of Diane's childhood and adulthood. Finally the facts came out. Diane had been sexually abused by a cousin when she was a child in Mexico. The parents said "only a few times" and had put the issue to rest. Then she was raped as a teenager in an LA high school bathroom.

Diane's parents were embarrassed and made her stay in the house except for the time she spent in school. Her father admitted that he did punish her for allowing herself to be put into a situation where she was raped. He was angry and handled the situation badly. All the appropriate sources were contacted. Again the matter was laid to rest after several counseling sessions.

Diane finished school and then began a slow decline in functioning. She rarely went out of the house but did some babysitting for a couple next door. Things didn't look too bad except that her father still somehow thought she had some responsibility for the earlier rape.

Then she got pregnant and the parents didn't know that she was pregnant until she was 6 months along and her clothes didn't fit. Who was the father? No one knew. Dianna denied that she ever had sexual relations. She was "a virgin".

When the baby was born, Diane couldn't deny that he was there but she had absolutely no way of bonding with the infant. She admitted that she felt no joy and didn't know what to do with him. The nursing staff patiently showed her how to hold and feed him but they remarked that she was not happy or warm or curious about the child. The way that she spoke about him was as if he suddenly appeared and she was amazed and shocked. She was unable to care for him and her parents took over.

This is a real and a dramatic case that we present in order to show that the effects of victimization on women are both physiological and psychological. The fact is that abuse has long-term harmful effects in many domains of health that are transmitted to the next generation. According to a lot of research, *a history of victimization is associated with maternal depressive symptoms and with harsh parenting style.* The mother's ability to read and express and regulate her own and her baby's emotional signals are impacted by the abuse. The worse case scenario is when the mother has been victimized both in childhood and adulthood; like our client, Diane. This is known as added risk. The kinds of relationships that the pregnant woman has had in the past and in the present will affect the development of emotional skills in the unborn child.

As we look for groups of women who fall into high-risk categories we should remember that the numbers of women who are in jails and prisons is increasing dramatically. Most incarcerated women are young and many are pregnant. The cumulative effects of incarceration and pregnancy lead to very high levels of infant mortality, intrauterine growth retardation, pre term labor and other problems.

In this captive population, the complex interrelationships between drug use, sexual/physical abuse, psychological problems, and poverty can be seen first hand. Multiple factors combine to make prison pregnancy a dreadful experience for the mother and the infant who is usually taken away at birth.

A program called WIAR for pregnant prisoners with histories of drug or alcohol abuse proved that even in this highest risk population, the results of early intervention during the pregnancy had good "birth outcomes" for infant and for mother. Due to funding limitations there were no available programs after the women were released and the long-term results are not available as yet.

In high-risk situations, intervention during pregnancy is a positive step. We have now looked at the various factors that can contribute to making you a parent with intact emotional skills and one who sets the stage for an emotionally wise and secure child. The very best thing you can do for your child is to enjoy your pregnancy as much as possible — feel the joy of being the carrier of new life and the amazing intimacy of nourishing a living being inside you. Even those who have had a difficult time reading and expressing emotion are often bowled over by the intensity of love they feel for their unborn child, which only grows more at birth.

You move up from this Step prepared with information that will guide you towards helping your child develop self control skills and ultimately, emotional intelligence. Understanding your own emotional states and triggers, your strengths and weaknesses will empower you to teach and to practice self control skills. And you will be actively teaching these life lessons to your child or to others if you are a parent, a teacher or a care provider.

Because of the fact that this step in developing self control brings up very important concepts for parents and other child involved individuals we recommend the following:

1. Have a good knowledge of your own Comfort Zone; how it feels when you're in it and what it takes to get back into it when you are on the roller coaster. Remember that this comfort zone is a state of awake, alert, awareness. It is a pleasant and motivating emotional state.
2. Take the time to keep track of your feelings during the day.

3. Reduce stress as soon as you experience it.

4. Remain in your own Comfort Zone as much as possible.

5. Take a look at the Resource section at the end of this book and review the safe and informative internet sites and teaching tips provided for you.

A Sneak Preview: Imagine your child 5 years from now. Close your eyes and there is your 5 year old child with all of the strengths he could possibly have because of your efforts during pregnancy. Now he may not be perfect, he may well be far from the ideal child but those abilities that you see are part of what you gave him. And if you look you will find abilities that reflect his pre birth environment and the attention you paid to your pregnancy. Perhaps he responds to music and you played music to relax during yourself pregnancy? Or maybe you did a lot of enjoyable activities and he seems to be in a good mood a lot of the time? It could be that you spent some time during your pregnancy just day dreaming wonderful things about your baby. In these and other ways you did try to keep yourself in a Comfort Zone and it did impact your child's development every time that you were in a positive balanced state.

Step Two: Birth to 2 months

Finding Comfort Zones & Self-Control

Marla and Dan hover over the crib of their 2 week old little boy. They stay very quiet after having found that he was disturbed by their conversation. The baby sleeps. Then the little face flushes and rosebud mouth opens in a wail.

"Hey little Mike I thought you were resting"
Dan says

"Wait a minute maybe he'll settle down. "
Marla says hopefully

The baby's cry gets louder. His face reddens and the tiny limbs thrash around.

"OK how long do you want to wait?" says
Dan asks Marla. "I'm late for work"

Mom picks the baby up as their 17-month-old, Jill, toddles in to see what the fuss is all about.

"Mommy?" the little girl says. "Why is baby crying?" Her own little face has a concerned look.

Dan looks down at the toddler and then over to the baby. He takes Jill's hand and leads her out of the room to play with her.

Marla leans over and scoops the baby into her arms. "Yes," she murmurs, "you're certainly different than your big sister."

She continues to hold the infant until he settles down and then tucks him into the crib. She closes the drapes over the window, shuts off the light and steps outside. At the door she pauses, hearing perhaps the beginning of another cry. But Mike is quiet. And yet she knows that this little infant will be calling out again very soon. "No rest for the weary." Marla whispers to herself.

You remember Marla and Dan? These parents are entering Step 2 and it is a brand new experience. We'll be following them throughout the book to see how they handle things. Once again it seems as though they did what they needed to do to bring this baby into his comfort zone. Another lesson taught and learned. It looked easy the first time they interacted with him but things look a bit different now. The parents look a bit more frazzled and the baby, well he appears to be more on the "temperamental" side.

This little baby is indeed different from her first infant, as Marla noted. This one came with a different set of genes, a different way of behaving right from the get go. And the reality is that his unique temperament will have a lot to do with the teaching and the learning of self-control.

For years, parents knew that some babies were harder to deal with than others. Some infants had tendencies to cry more intensely and more often, to be awake more, to move around more, to sense changes around them more quickly and to respond to these changes with passion. At one extreme, parents have referred to such babies as "difficult" and "temperamental." This would be just fine except for the fact that many of them stay that way. At the other extreme we have the docile, sleepy heads that need to be prodded in order to feed. And somewhere in the middle, of course, the "perfect" baby who cries but not excessively, and is awake for feeding and playing and just seems so well-balanced.

The terms that have been used in the past for temperamental styles are timid, bold, upbeat and melancholy. Babies fit more easily into categories that describe them by levels of excitability and this is more useful for our purposes; hence we have the range of temperaments from very easily excited through not easily excited. Babies fall somewhere along this range and have **comfort zones that vary enormously**. These comfort zones are important and parents are hoping to find them as a base for teaching self-control skills.

Looking at another case, Leslie was born full term, an 8 pound little girl. Her mother, Sara took her home from the hospital in 3 days and as soon as she put her into the new, shiny crib the baby started crying. Nothing seemed to soothe her, not holding, feeding, changing, singing or massage. Sara spent 4 sleepless nights trying to get it together. Then she called the doctor and received the interesting news.

Even though Leslie is a healthy, full term baby it is still a fact that inside the brains of some newborns the chemical soothing mechanisms *are not wired in place until the third month*. At least 25% of newborns need the extra time and effort to get into a comfort zone. Yet these little ones are completely normal by any standards.

After talking with the doctor, Sara groaned when she put down the phone. She was relieved and yet…the idea of 2 more months made her a bit queasy.

Leslie and Little Mike are like many babies in that they fit into the moderately temperamental category. Not easy infants. Interacting with them may be more labor-intensive for parents and it may be more taxing for the infants at times. And yet, they do have their Comfort Zone although it may be easily disturbed and hard to find at times.

There have been more studies recently on the connection between Comfort Zones, the temperament of newborns and how this impacts the developing capacity for self-control. One way is fairly straight forward and that is that babies who are difficult to arouse or difficult to calm can make parents feel frustrated, or angry or unloved. Parents then respond to these babies differently and may over or under react and misjudge where the baby's comfort zone is. Sherry's case shows us how this happens.

Sherry has a 3 week-old little boy. She is only 20 years old and will be raising him on her own. She wanted to be a great mother and to give the baby opportunities that she never had but somehow this infant doesn't seem to like her. In this third week of being a Mom she is exhausted from being awake almost 24 hours at a time in order to keep him happy. Yet he cries. And she feels that it is because she isn't doing it well enough. So she increases her efforts, doing everything from playing "up" music to singing and dancing around with him in her arms, and caressing him. Still he cries and it even seems that he cries more. She is heart broken, tired and unhappy.

In yet another case, an infant who is **not** easily stimulated may seem distant or depressed. Parents may respond to this by trying to push him to respond or by leaving him alone because he is a "quiet" baby.

John is a tiny newborn who lies in his crib in what seems like a deep sleep. He is a thin baby but healthy. His face looks like that of a wrinkled old man. John's parents are moving to a smaller apartment since his Dad lost his job. There is a lot going on around him in terms of packing and arguing but he sleeps on. He's so quiet that his mother has to arouse him rather noisily for feeding. Sometimes he falls asleep while nursing. John's parents are so preoccupied with the moving and financial crisis that they are just relieved that he's "not a problem" When Dad picks him up John doesn't open his eyes and his father thinks that the baby isn't ready for interaction. He decides to give it one more try and holds John up, supporting his neck. Then he loudly calls the baby's name and sings a rousing baseball song. That wakes the infant up and he cries briefly. Dad puts him back in the crib feeling a bit better about his son.

Parents have to be good judges of their infant's temperament and comfort zones from the get go even though things are changing rapidly. Research has demonstrated that when parents understand and work with the baby's unique level of sensitivity from day 1, the quality of their relationship is better at age 12. And so by understanding the infant's temperament and working to find his comfort zone you prepare him to be in that alert, awake and aware state that makes teaching and learning much easier.

Working with the infant to find a Comfort Zone means more than constantly soothing him. Many books have been written on techniques for soothing, quieting the infant. But the brain grows through challenges and these have to be within the infant's ability to handle them and the parent's ability to bring him back into comfortable balance. What parents are looking for is a state of calm attention in the infant. The Triple A state of awake, alert and aware and this state is a flashing signal to parents that the child is ready to absorb new lessons.

Getting into the baby's nervous system we must imagine that his behaviors of crying, thrashing around do not always signal "pain". This is what we as adults *think* that it is. For the baby, short periods of fussiness may be his first attempts to express emotions in general. And he hasn't a clue about how to show what he feels. So we mustn't dampen all of these expressions of feeling. Finding the infant's comfort zone so that you can bring him out of a long, hard, crying jag relieves him of stress and has a beneficial effect upon the brain in physical terms. Basic brain data shows that leaving an infant in a chronic state of what is called "hyper arousal" or over-excitedness is damaging to brain cells and can lead to severe problems in teaching him how to control emotions and behavior in the next steps.

Within the first few days, parents *can take their baby's temperament as easily as they take his temperature*. Experts in the field of neonatology have found that there are several basic things to look for in terms of temperament.

These are: How the baby looks (color tone), how it moves and how it sounds (crying etc). Parents can watch for changes in these indicators while the baby is fully asleep, awake (not excited but aroused), and when he is very excited (crying, thrashing around). These three states of being will guide you to your baby's Comfort Zone.

Many parents find it easier to evaluate the baby for the first time when he or she is asleep. A simple list is helpful for this.

Evaluation Tools for Taking the Infant's Temperament

Notes for **color** when baby is asleep, awake, very excited,
Notes for **body movement** when baby is asleep, awake, very excited,
Notes for **vocalization** when baby is awake and very excited
Marla and Dan have the notes on Mike. Mike's **sleeping** temperament is: pale skin with faint flush on cheeks, quiet limbs, no vocalization. Mikes **awake** temperament is: rosy skin, movement in arms and legs, *soft crying* from time to time. Mike's **overexcited** (irritable) state is: red face, thrashing limbs loud crying.

43

This guides Marla and Dan with the periods of time, small as they may be, when he is most capable of interacting with his teaching, nurturing parents.

Next it is useful to see how many episodes your baby spends in his over excited, awake state. A check off list near the crib will help. You simply put a mark each time the baby is in the crying, thrashing around state where you feel the need to do something. Now see if doing the techniques that we describe below can change the chart.

Mike's bedside chart before techniques   *Mike's chart after techniques*
Irritable awake: 111111111111 (12)   *11111111 (8)*

Once parents have an idea of the baby's temperament they can use any of the techniques for soothing and for stimulating that we discuss later on in this chapter. It's not always easy to find the baby's comfort zone but if you manage to get to it some of the time you are doing a great job. **This is the milestone for this step.**

In all of this discussion about your baby's temperament it is important for the parents (who are the teachers and models for the infant) to once again take stock of their own feelings about the baby in his or her varied states. *Childbirth can change things for parents.* This includes their moods, their expectations and their stress levels. As early as the first 24 hours of life, parents begin to form opinions of their newborns. These opinions are, of course based partly on the temperament of the baby and these opinions can last a very long time. Your emotions will be translated into behavior and definitely felt by the infant.

> *Dr. P is an attractive young pathologist who waited to have her first child until she and her husband were well established. And they are established. The savings account is full. They have a large home with many bedrooms and bathrooms. They have a state of the art kitchen and a backyard with trees and a sauna. Dr .P interviewed nannies for many months and has one on call at the moment that she comes home with the baby.*

44

After the delivery, Dr .P was surrounded with friends and family. Her daughter was healthy but she wasn't feeling very happy. For a few days she waited for the joy, the overwhelming sense of something that new mothers have. Everyone told her that she had it, they could see it in her face. But they were so wrong. She wasn't feeling anything but tired.

And there was a big problem with her husband. Now that the baby was born he wanted her to leave the infant with the nanny and get back into the groove. He acted like she was normal although she knew that something was way off. Everyone was asking her over and over again "Aren't you pleased? This is exactly what you wanted! Aren't you feeling happy and lucky?"

Then there was her job. Then there were colleagues sending flowers and cards showing beaming mothers and their rosy smiling babies. The TV commercials made it even worse.

For a couple of weeks she faked joy and satisfaction. It made her feel like a liar. She returned to work when the baby was one month old and picked up the pieces as best she could. But the feelings never did go away and she was guilty about it for a long, long time. She was ashamed of not having the "right" feelings and this kept her from getting help.

Dr. P is not alone in her emotional experiences. For some parents, after waiting and hoping and preparing, there is an intense let down feeling after the baby is born. As *uncomfortable and embarrassing* as this feeling may be it deserves attention. The earlier these emotions are identified, the faster you can get the help you need.

As soon as the baby is born, it is useful to look at your feelings about the new arrival. It is often the case that people who are not so ' directly involved in the parenting can get an objective view of the parent's opinions of the newborn. So find someone to answer these questions.

Early Post Partum Evaluation Tool for Parents

Answer as honestly as you can	Yes	No	Not Sure
Do you feel comfortable holding your baby?			
Do you find your infant to be cuddly?			
Do you thank that your baby is already high maintenance?			
Do you like the way your baby looks?			
Do you wish your baby had a different disposition?			
Do you think that you are doing a good job parenting at this early time?			
Are you worrying about your own feelings during the day?			
Do you like the way your baby smells?			
Are you disgusted by the baby's bowel movements or other bodily functions?			
Are you upset when someone gives you advice aboutparenting?			
Do you pick up the baby even before it cries?			
Are you frequently comparing your baby to others?			
Do you find yourself examining the baby's fingers and toes?			

	Yes	No	Not Sure
Do you find yourself singing or talking to the baby?			
Do you talk about the baby in a positive way to others?			

Rating the questionnaire: If you answered 'Yes' or 'Uncertain' to questions 3,5,7,9,10,and 12 you will definitely benefit from doing some healthy work on yourself. Even though caring for this baby is taxing, your feelings count too and will impact your parenting skills in the area of self-control. Please see our index for resources and you will find other new mothers in exactly the same situation. You are not a bad mother and you are not alone. These early problems may not put you into the "depressed" category but they do indicate that something is going on.

Evaluation Tools for Others in the situation

	Always	Never
Does the parent hold the baby close to the body?		
Does the parent smile when holding the baby?		
Does the parent say positive things about the baby?		
Does the parent make loving talk to the baby?		
Does the parent try to make eye contact with the baby?		

If you answer 'Never' to 3 or more of these questions it may be time to ask the parent if you can help. Staying quiet usually doesn't do anyone any good. So try and not blame the new parent and step in there.

If you find that you as a parent feel bad or sad about the way things are going with the baby it is time to take some action. We say this with emphasis because of the fact that if parent's feelings of helplessness, sadness or frustration are not addressed they may become worse. A great deal of research has been done on post partum sadness and depression (mothers) and we have seen fathers in unhappy states as well. The "baby blues" as these studies have found do not always evaporate and may worsen if the baby is a demanding one.

Sad parents and angry parents of newborns relate to their infants in unhealthy ways most of the time. Parents who are unhappy may actually perceive the infant as sad or troublesome when the baby is just doing his own thing. Frustrated parents are also likely to have negative opinions about the baby and may even loose patience with the infant. Parents who cannot manage their own emotions and behavior are inadequate teachers for their children. If they can't find a Comfort Zone, how can they help their infants into that balanced, positive domain?

It is no longer considered "normal" to be very depressed for any length of time after the birth of a baby or very anxious for that matter. We have offered tests for stress in the preceding chapter and how here is a useful evaluation tool for parents.

Evaluation Tool for Depression After Birth of Baby

	Often	Rarely
1. Do you feel sad, weepy, and unhappy?		
2. Are you motivated to care for yourself?		
3. Are you motivated to care for the baby?		
4. Do you feel alone?		
5. Do you have trouble sleeping (getting to sleep or staying asleep?		
6. Are you staying to yourself and avoiding others?		
7. Do you think about worrisome things?		
8. Do you regret what you've done after doing it?		
9. Do you get irritated easily?		

If you are in the "always" category 5 or more times it is important that you seek counseling. For those in mild depression we suggest the kind of "mood work" that you can do at home.

There are self-help strategies that really work to help you change your thoughts and your moods. One of them is an easy beginning exercise:

1. List your good qualities (physical, emotional, social, creative etc) as in "I am healthy, I am creative in cooking, I care about people, I have goals for my child, I am patient, I...)

2. Say these statements aloud give examples of each one. As in "I care about people. Yesterday I read about war in the Middle East and I felt badly for the people in that country.) Or "I am creative in cooking. Last week I read a receipt and I am planning on how to creatively adapt it for my husband who is picky, picky)

3. Now, take a few minutes regularly during the day to remember the list

4. Put one thought into practice even if it is very simple; as in I will begin to think of a letter to write to the paper about the consequences of war for the people in other countries.

Here is your milestone. Now that you are more comfortable or on your way to being in your comfort zone it is time to help the baby find his comfort zone. The truth is that when you as a parent feel good even the most difficult baby is more manageable.

And now back to your baby. Techniques for soothing and stimulating your baby are found in many books. The ones that you choose will depend upon the temperament of your own infant. And you will have to test them out after you know the distress signals that your baby shows (red face, thrashing body yelling etc).

Creative soothing techniques include; music, massage and swaddling the infant firmly in a soft blanket. Your baby may be comforted easily by the sound of your voice, your smell, a quiet room or the feel of your fingers brushing against his skin.

Marla has found that baby Mike is most comfortable when the

environment around him is fairly quiet and the lights are low. When she takes him out she uses the baby carriage that has a hood so that she can modify the light for him. She also tells people to whisper and not babble loudly into his face. And yet she doesn't fret when he gets restless. She tries to comfort him before it gets too bad.

Creative stimulating techniques include brightening up the infant's environment with shapes, colors and sounds. Two techniques used by the experts are the following:

1. The ball exercise: Hold the infant on your lap with his head towards your knees. This way you can use one hand to hold him and the other to bring a brightly colored ball in front of his face (not too close). Then move the ball slowly to the right and then slowly to the left. Your baby may track this object attentively.

2. The rattle exercise: this is the same format using a soft rattle near the baby's left and then right ear. Too loud a sound will startle the infant so be careful.

3. The voice exercise: with one arm supporting the baby on your lap raise his head and shoulders slightly. Put your lips close to his left ear leaving enough room for him to move his head and speak softly. See if your baby responds with interest by trying to orient himself to your voice.

4. The combo exercise: use your voice and face as the signals for the infant by putting your face within range of his vision and speaking softly. Now let him follow your face and voice to the left and to the right.

Let your baby's responses or lack of responses guide you in how intensely you use your voice, the rattle and any other stimuli. If by chance the infant becomes too excited and begins to cry you know that you have reached his limits for adjusting to new things at this time. He'll become more and more able to cope with new experiences as he grows…as his brain capacity grows!

This has been an important experience for parent and infant. As a parent, you can take your infant's temperament reading almost as easily as you take his temperature. When you continue to take his temperament and to work within his Comfort Zones you regulate his fluctuating emotions until he can do it himself. You are teaching him what it feels like to be balanced and when you think about it, how could he experience this inner feeling without you?

The baby's milestone is that he or she can be helped into a Comfort Zone. This important step will lead you directly into the next phase. Remember that you will be taking his temperament as you go along, and you can do this at any age with any child. You can see what excites your youngster, what calms him and most importantly what temperamental state he functions well in.

You will move up from this Step with information that prepares you to develop your child's self control skills and reach his highest potential in terms of emotional intelligence. The Comfort Zone is the key to the infant's learning about what a healthy emotional balance **feels** like. We have seen how the parent's interactions with the infant bring him into this wonderful state as often as possible. In the next steps you will see how this balanced state empowers the brain to learn new self-control skills. It is important to try and do the following on a routine basis:

1. Take the time to look at and listen to your child of any age and identify when they are in their Comfort Zones; the *Awake, Alert, Aware state.*

2. Look around you at your partner, friends and others to see when they are in or out of their comfort zones.

3. Take your own temperament reading several times a day

A Sneak Preview. Imagine your child 5 years from now. There she is and you recognize that look on her face, don't you? It's that comfortable look she gets when she is relaxed and happy. She's playing with her friends and they really like to be around her. This expression tells you that she has a comfort zone and now you realize that she is in that awake, alert and aware state a lot of the time. Thanks to you she is able to maintain an emotional balance and she'll be able to learn a great many other things in that comfortable state as she gets older.

Step Three: Faces, Voices and Self-Control

On this particular morning, Marla is getting Jill and 3 month old Mike ready for a trip to the store. She's done this before and she is making the trip as fast and focused as she can. Jill babbles excitedly as her mom ties her shoelaces,

"Store...toys?"

As she dresses little Jill, Mike is fussing in the baby chair that sits on the floor below them. He's testing the safety straps, kicking his legs and getting restless. Jill looks down at him and says in her soft, sweet voice, "Baby crying?"

Marla lets the little girl go over to baby Mike. She's noticed that recently the baby seems to calm down when Jill is close by. Not too close however, he still doesn't like being crowded.

Jill crouches near the infant and he stops momentarily as her face swims into his line of vision. In that one perfect and tiny space of time the two children look at each other.

Mike's eyes open wide as he focuses on Jill. There is a gleam of happiness in his eyes. His body is quiet, but not relaxed. Then Jill moves her head to the side and the baby follows her face. His legs move once in a kind of spasm of joy.

Marla watches in fascination as Mike's mouth opens and his lips turn up in a grin.

Jill giggles and the baby splutters wetly. "See, Mom. Baby talking" Jill says proudly.

What could it feel like to be inside this infant's body, inside his nervous system as this wonderful experience happens? One can only imagine the feeling of being strapped into a hard plastic thing on the floor and out of the line of sight of two important people. Way, way up there is a lot of action. Ah yes, now Mike can see them and hear their familiar sounds. But they're too far up and away right now. Suddenly he feels a surge of some kind of emotion as a little face; a familiar face comes into view. It's Jill getting down right near him. This is a shape he can't name but he's riveted to it. A good sensation courses though him even though it takes some effort to keep this shape in focus. Then the face moves. He holds it in view and his movement causes more excitement. As he tracks Jill's face with his head moving right and then left. Wow! What an experience for this little brain. A roller coaster ride that felt pretty good along the way.

If Marla is doing a temperament reading on Mike she recognizes that this face- to- face exercise for her baby has brought him into a positive comfort zone. In fact, all three of them are in a balanced positive state.

And yet, there is so much more that this face- to- face interaction has done inside Mike's active brain. His brain has developed quickly and he is ready for new learning about self control. *The lessons at this stage will help him to read emotional expressions.* This is one of the most valuable things that a parent can teach in the realm of self-control as we will see.

If we pause and fast forward a bit into the future we can see Mike at the age of 5 focusing intently upon the face of his teacher in school and paying attention to what he sees there. We can also envision him looking at his little friend's emotional expressions and reading them for clues, for information.

Here is the key connection between faces and the development of self- control: the human expressive face is full of information that youngsters need to focus upon and read in order for them to manage their inner emotions and react appropriately. What we see on the human face is a multitude of signals. These signals tell us, for example, if the person is happy and it is safe for us to approach or if we should gear up for running away. These are simple and yet eloquent signals. They are meant to get our attention, engage our emotions and trigger us to do something.

For babies, this begins process with the very early face to face interactions with parents and significant people in their environment. Welcome to Step 2.

Now let's go back to Marla and her kids.

In the store, some hours later on, Jill is walking behind Marla and the baby. It is pretty crowded and the shoppers bump into Jill occasionally because she's looking at toys and not the people around her. Suddenly she steps on the toes of a man who is wearing sandals. She looks up and his face is red with anger, eyes flashing and mouth open to say something. She focuses on the mad expression for a moment. It rivets her. Jill has seen angry faces but this one scares her terribly. She feels something bad inside. This discomfort is not a good thing. She doesn't like the bad feeling. Jill knows what will make her feel better. She runs for her mother, tugs on her hand and relaxes when Marla looks down at her. Jill is a good face reader. The angry face that made her feel bad worked to propel her in the direction of safety...her mother. What would have happened if she misread or ignored his expression? What could have happened if she didn't know how to find her source of comfort?

The expressive human face stirs up feelings in all of us. We are all wired, from birth to attend more to the shape of a human face than towards objects. Yet, the reading of the expressions in the face and our ability to use that information is learned. Within the baby brain, positive face- to- face experiences with the mother actually cause positive chemicals to surge in the brain. And negative experiences can be damaging if they are repeated and intense.

During the early months as your infant is adjusting to the world, you want him or her to learn to read face expressions that are primarily positive and that stimulate and soothe him within his particular comfort zone.

This is the milestone you are looking for.

Now let's get back to Marla.

Marla has a friend who also has a young baby. She visited

Irma one day when Dan had the kids with him. Irma had never been the high energy out-going, bubbly type of woman but when she answered the door Marla saw that she looked bad. She was wearing an old robe, her hair hanging limply and the house smelled stale. Irma gave her a weak hug said "Hi" but looked down at the floor.

"Where's the baby?" asked Marla.

"In the other room." Irma responded, gesturing with her hand to a dark room off to the side.

"How is she?" Marla questioned.

"Ok, I guess." Irma sighed and sat down on the sofa. The baby began to cry but Irma sat staring at her hands. "She'll stop eventually." That was all she said.

Marla went into the bedroom and saw the infant, red-faced and uncovered. She picked her up and brought her over to Irma who held the baby loosely on her lap. The infant kept crying.

Irma rocked her body jerkily back and forth for a minute. She looked miserable. Then she said. "It'll get better soon. I'm just having the baby blues, you know? Everyone tells me to get on with it and not worry."

Marla saw that her friend's face was flat and almost expressionless as she talked. There wasn't even the hint of joy, not a gleam of delight in holding her baby. This face- to- face had no good feeling to it at all. And the baby kept crying. Marla felt almost relieved that the baby was held in a way that she couldn't see the look on her mother's face. "It would be enough to turn anyone off or make them cry", she thought to herself.

Face expressions convey emotional information. And the baby at this age is trying to learn to read them. Depression, anxiety and anger show themselves in facial expressions as well as body language and vocalizations. Parents who are sad, tense angry may well be able to keep their voices down but their feelings are communicated in their facial expressions.

After reading this, Marla runs into the bathroom and stands in front of the mirror. She's been avoiding this because she knows that she doesn't look "her best". Now she is wondering what she looks like to Mike and Jill. What do they see in her face expressions? She is tired, of course, and somewhat tense but as soon as she thinks about the kids a funny grin breaks out over her face. The mirror reflects a tired but happy and loving face. That's what is inside and that's what she is showing to her children.

Marla hadn't looked in the mirror in this fashion in quite a while. Most adults give a cursory glance or focus on certain parts of their faces while putting on make-up or shaving. In fact, in this high tech world some adults don't have to go out of the house and interact with other people on a face- to- face basis. And adults can loose touch with what face expressions signal. The danger in this is that adults may fail to look at their children's face expressions and be unaware of their own.

Take for example, the open-mouthed, wide-eyed look of pure fear on the human face, or the snarling red face of anger. These are expressions that are meant to grab our attention, stimulate feelings and guide behavior. Do you approach someone who looks like he wants to hurt you? And this is all learned.

Not all children are able to learn these important lessons. Many of them wind up being diagnosed with a serious disorder at a later age and their lack of self control skills is painfully obvious.

There are new studies that show that children who are later found to have ADHD (Attention Deficit Disorder) have a difficult time with picking up subtle changes in face expressions, gestures and other emotional signals.

One of your authors has worked with many ADHD children and their parents. What was astounding with these kids and parents was that during sessions with the family, the parents did not have eye contact with their children. Nor did the kids look at their parents. It took a great deal of encouragement to teach families how, when, and why looking directly at faces and face expressions was important.

In yet another area, kids with Autism do not look at faces from early infancy. The underlying cause of this is probably a combination of heredity and early parental interaction factors. Professionals who work with autistic kids and their families find that teaching face-reading does benefit these kids. Emotional expressions that are conveyed by the human face are nutritious food for the infant's brain.

There are ways for parents to improve their own abilities to read face expressions so that they read their infant's signals and teach this skill in a natural manner.

Reading Evaluation Tool: How well do you read?

Answer	yes	no
1. I look at people's faces on a regular, daily basis		
2. I am more comfortable talking on the phone than in person		
3. I think that face expressions do reflect feelings		
4. When I see an angry expression I want to distance myself		
5. I've been taught to smile when I am sad or angry		
6. I can usually tell if a smile is not sincere		
7. I've been told that my face reflects how I feel and I like that.		
8. I enjoy watching people's face expressions		
9. When I read I imagine how these character's faces look		
10. The family I grew up in showing respect by not looking directly at people?		
11. I think pets have face expressions too?		
12. My smile is my best facial feature.		
13. I think that if someone looks at me they are reading my thoughts		

Looking at the above questions, if you answered "yes" to questions 1, 3,6,7,8,9,11 and 12 you have pretty good reading capacity. In case you answered "no" to many of the questions or simply want to be sure that your reading skills are good, please do the exercises below. Practice can make perfect.

Exercise in Reading Faces

1. Stand in front of a mirror. Try to make a face that expresses happiness. Then try expressions for anger and sadness. Get subtler and do faces that suggest contentment, anxiety and surprise.

2. Enlist a partner. Make the expressions of anger, fear and joy. Does he or she recognize these expressions?

Exercises with the Baby: Mirroring

1. When your baby is in his or her awake but not excited state hold him on your lap face up with his head at your knees.

2. Put your close enough for his particular vision

3. Mirror the expression on his face as best you can. Does he focus on you? You may try to move your face to the left and right to bring up his attention.

4. Continue to reflect his expressions watching for his response in the changes in his expression; the gleam in his eyes, color tone, limb movement, vocalizations.

5. Make your happy and surprised faces and note his response as above.

6. When he becomes very excited, stop and bring him into his relaxed state.

7. If there is little no response you may try moving in closer, and doing this exercise on a regular basis when he is in a relaxed state. Remember to keep it light and keep it positive. Some infants may need soft sounds in addition to the face expressions just to get started. You can add vocalizations for these babies who may have keener hearing than sight at this point, or they may simply prefer tuning in to your voice.

8. Keep track of your infant's growing ability to focus on your face and to respond to different face expressions. If he is unable to focus or is unresponsive after a few weeks have the doctor check out his vision.

You have a milestone here. Your baby is now reading on the most important level of all; the emotional level.

Fathers often do have a great deal of influence over children at this exciting stage.

> **Dan knows what sounds and face expressions set Mike into a happy orbit. He likes making all kinds of strange noises and watching the baby make his own sounds. .Right now he's making a soft strangling sound as he holds the baby on his lap. Marla can hear the two of them from the kitchen. It sounds pretty odd.**
>
> **"Ah ug la!" Dan says in a happy tone of voice. She can't quite hear Mike but he must be saying something because Dan is laughing.**

These early sound interactions will also add to the infant's ability to harness the power of the emotional roller coaster. It may not be language yet, but Mike is learning how to express himself in sound. His babbling is the building block of speech. When parents encourage babbling, or any of the infant's earliest noises they help to set the stage for expressive language. From everything that we know, being able to verbally express feelings and thoughts enables us to control and to regulate our emotions.

If we could peek into Mike's brain at this point, we would see that there is awesome development going on in the systems that support language. As his brain grows so do his learning abilities and Dan is right there stimulating them. Two month old babies can remember word sounds. Hopefully there are lots and lots of word sounds all around them.

And now a word about baby's who cannot hear. They have been found to babble with their hands. They talk with gestures and can be as good as hearing children with expressing and managing their emotions and behavior.

As you enjoy the face- to- face and the babbling interactions with your baby you push his brain development further. The milestones for this step may seem to be quite trivial; *the baby focuses upon your face, responds to your face and voice stimulation.* Yet, you can't get more important than this for the development of the most special capacity of all. Your child's ability to look at and try to understand face and voice communication will propel him into the next phase. It will help him to learn all of the rest of the lessons and to climb the steps towards self- control. And you are at the controls because right now your baby is paying attention to you. You, the parents, are still the one's who make him comfortable and read his temperament. In the next few steps your child will come a bit closer to learning how to manage his own roller coaster of emotions.

You will move up from this Step with amazing information that will help your child develop self control skills and then reach the precious goal of emotional intelligence. From a child's vantage point, the parent is a whole world of sights, sensations and sounds. They learn from this world of emotional experiences in ways that are simple and yet vitally important. And they are learning lessons in emotional communication that will enable them to manage their feelings and their behavior. When your infant gazes at you and listens to your voice just imagine her paying attention to the voice and face of her teacher in school. You, as a parent, want her to focus upon important face and voice expressions and not be distracted by lots of other stimuli. This is part of developing self control. In this regard it is vital to do the following:

1. Interact with your infant in a warm and comforting manner as much as possible.

2. Use your face, your voice and your touch to communicate joy and love.

3. Reward your child's emotional expressiveness with active attention: verbal or facial or a simple touch.

A Sneak Preview; Imagine your child 10 years from now. You can see her in a crowd of kids in the auditorium. There is a lot of noise and commotion as a teacher explains the importance of being safe in school. The lecture is all about how to prepare for emergencies such as fires and bombs and attacks. Many of the kids think it is silly. Your daughter is listening and she is focused upon the teacher's serious face. She knows from his voice and the look in his eyes that this is important. You taught her how to pay attention to face and voice expressions. Now that lesson will keep her safe in another situation where her life may depend upon it.

Step Four: Attachment and Self- Control

"It's time to play, kids!" Little Mike sits on Marla's lap holding tightly onto the fabric of her skirt. Across the room, another 7 month old is yelling and burying her face in her mother's shoulder. One infant has crawled into the center of the circle. He sits up. All eyes are focused upon this brave explorer. No other baby dares to compete.

This is day one of play group for babies. What fun for the mothers who want their kids to get together on the floor and interact with joy! Perhaps the kids will play ball or sing a song together. The mother of the wailing baby looks embarrassed and Marla can feel the rigidity in Mikes little body. He's looking around at the other babies and Moms.

Finally, after a few painful minutes the mother of crying infant says "She won't leave my arms since I tried having the babysitter watch her for a few hours last week."

"Really?" says the mother of the brave explorer "Little Brandon's been in day care since he was 6 weeks old. I had to go back to work. He has a sitter in the evenings when I'm on call at the hospital."

Little Brandon is crawling towards the open door. Just before he gets there his mother scoops him up and puts him back down in the middle of the floor.

Is this baby amazing or what! Brandon seems to have an edge on the whole process of developing self control! It almost looks as though he leaped up the Steps 2 at a time! Here he is in the company of strangers seemingly at ease, crawling forward to meet new challenges. The other babies well, they're babies! There they are clinging to Mom as though being in a completely new situation is a scary thing and they want Mom to make them feel better.

Let's peek inside Mike's mind and interpret his sensations.

"What are these strange faces? I don't know what they are. It's not a pleasant feeling. I only know the face of my Mom, her voice, her touch her smell. Ahhh. I have her right here. Feels good that I'm close to her. I'm going to stay put for now."

In reality, self -control isn't about being out there on your own at 7 months or 8 months. It's all about knowing that the person who can take you right to your comfort zone is close by.   Infants of Brandon and Mike's ages haven't had all the lessons yet on the subject of self-control and they still need an adult to help them get through the ups the downs the strange situations and the scary ones. So Brandon's behavior looks good from some aspects but skipping steps here is not the way to arrive at the goal.

What is crucial in this step is that the baby have very close ties or attachment to someone who makes him feel secure, feel comfortable when he's on a roller coaster ride of emotions and new experiences. From this secure attachment he or she will be equipped to sail forth into the phase of healthy exploration. That means taking the first step away from his comfort zone with the knowledge, the belief that he can get back fast if he needs to! **The secure- base type of exploration is the milestone of this step.**

What we can see from Mike's behavior that strikes a positive note is that he is close to Marla and she establishes his comfort zone. He clings but doesn't get frantic. Temperamentally we will say that he is at the edge of his comfort zone and probably if Marla went off somewhere he'd be out of control. The crying baby is not too far off the mark either. Some kids at this age are much more sensitive to separation from mother. Not a terrible flaw at this stage although it can be annoying for parents.

There is no "perfect" attachment style although many professionals use the secure attachment as a model. They all stress that secure and attached does not mean that the infant can go off on his own into new territory, nor does it mean that the baby is completely frazzled by any new experiences. At the end of this step you want your baby to be bonded to you and yet able to begin to explore his surroundings in a healthy way. Begin is the key word here. It is this balance between attachment and detachment (autonomy) that will launch him into step 5.

It is day two in the playgroup. The mothers have arranged to bring the kids to the same house in order to create a stable environment. Another mother and her baby boy have joined. That makes four sets; Marla and Mike, Barb and Brandon, Kate and Cathy (the crier) and new Nancy with little Bob. The mothers get comfy sitting in the circle on the floor with the kids on their laps. Nancy has her arms around Bob, Kate has a pacifier in Cathy's mouth and Brandon is already crawling into the circle. Mike looks up at Marla and she smiles. There is a gleam in his eyes that makes her catch her breath. He reaches up, touches her cheek and looks around.

Brandon crawls closer to the new kid, Bob, on his way to the door. Bob's mother says curtly "No! Go back to your Mommy that's what you're supposed to do." As she says this she tightens her grip on Bob who struggles in her arms. His face reddens. His mother squeezes a bit and says, "Hush Bobby, hush!" The baby starts to cry and she turns him towards her and holds his squirming body tightly against her. Suddenly he stops and seems to slump in her lap. "That's a good boy, take a nap." She says brightly.

Nancy is not a bad mother. Somehow she has developed certain ideas about security for her infant and these ideas are translated into the behavior above. This kind of interaction between mother and infant would be appropriate if they were in a situation where grave threats surrounded them. Then little Bob's crying and/or his emotional shut down could save his life. In this situation, however, his emotional and behavioral shut down is not at all suited to the social situation. It is, however, a response to his mother's engulfing him. He has done what he needed to do in order to somehow stop his discomfort.

Emotional and behavioral shut down or freezing is not the same as self- control. Babies will find ways to getting out of uncomfortable situations if their mothers/fathers do not help them in healthy ways. At this age, yelling, struggling, or shut down are the only ways these kids have to stop the roller coaster as it heads towards the cliffs. And it works for a short time. The danger is that yelling, struggling and freezing may continue to be used by these kids as they grow up.

Day three in play group.

On the third day in the play group some interesting things are happening. Mike is in the circle with Brandon and here comes Cathy, with her pacifier securely in her mouth. The pacifier was a brilliant idea on her mother's part and the baby is right in her comfort zone while beginning to explore. Pacifier and mom, what could be better? The babies seem to stay pretty close to their Moms and even look around for them from time to time.

At one point Brandon's mother receives a page. Surprisingly Brandon looks around in alarm when he hears the sound.

"I'll be right back" Barb says to the group. "I have to call the hospital." She leaves and

Brandon sits very still for a minute. A flash of concern appears on his face and then it's gone. When Barb comes back she tries to pick him up and he kicks out wildly, pushing away from her. She shrugs it off and sits down. Brandon makes a few moves close to her but stays towards the center of the circle.

All the babies are getting fussy and tired. Playtime is over. They crawl into their Mom's laps. All except Brandon who starts to wail in the middle of the circle. His mother picks him up and carries him crying out of the room.

And so we see that this little child has no healthy way to soothe himself all by himself. He is still too young and still dependent on an adult to soothe, to stimulate and to bring him back to his Comfort Zone. It's still the parent who should be the source of his security and comfort while allowing the baby some room for exploration. .

The milestone at this stage is that the baby is comfortable doing some exploring and yet knows how to get back to his comfort zone…his Mom or the adult who takes care of him. The capacity of the child to feel comfortable at a distance from his caretaker (his Comfort Zone provider) and believe that he can get back is a leap up the steps to self- control.

Day Four in Playgroup.

And here we are. Mike and Cathy are in the circle looking at each other. Cathy looks different. The pacifier has been left in Mom's lap. The babies stare at each other. Mike touches Cathy's curly red hair. She touches his nose. Their attention is drawn to little Bob who has crawled out of Mom's lap. He stays very close to Mom at all times. Then in comes Brandon with his babysitter. She's young and smiling and looks happy to be there. She sits down and Brandon lets her kiss and hug him while she introduces herself.

Towards the end of play group, Mike, Cathy and Brandon are roaming around each other playing with the little toys that are in the center of the circle. Brandon looks back at his sitter. They share a smile. Little Bob hasn't strayed far from his mother's lap. Of all the babies, he looks unhappy. When his mother talks he crawls away from her and when she is quiet he quickly crawls back to her and huddles in her lap. He almost looks confused if a baby of 8 months can express confusion by his face expressions and body movements.

We could say that Mike, Cathy and Brandon are able to maintain some kind of a Comfort Zone without their caretaker's right next to them. This is an important step in being able to manage their very own emotions. They have the inner belief that they can get back into a balanced situation and are therefore free to explore a bit.

Watching Brandon we can see that an infant can attach to someone other than the parent. This important person can teach the lessons of emotion and behavior control when the parent is for whatever reason, not available. Hopefully, Brandon's babysitter will remain in his life for the rest of the steps.

There is another amazing lesson to be learned from one of these kids and mothers in the play group. Crying Cathy is a great example of how parents boost an infant's sense of security by being creative and by being stable and reassuring even when the child is a mess! This is how kids learn that they are secure with you even when they make a mistake. The parent at this stage tolerates what is called negative emotion with ease and with creative thinking. The pacifier is a good example of saying to the child at this age;

"I know that you are feeling uncomfortable around these new faces and voices. I'm going to help you out so you will know how to do it for yourself one day. Here's a hand up the step, little one"

And what about Bob? How is he going to climb the rest of the steps? What Bob shows in his emotions and behavior is that he is not sure if his mother provides security or smothering. In this case, the source of his comfort is also a source of discomfort. We can sense his confusion in a situation where his natural urges are to explore and yet he doesn't know if he can get back into a comfort zone afterwards. If this becomes a learned pattern, then we can imagine Bob being uncertain if he can manage his own roller coaster of emotions later on.

When a child misses this step in the development of emotion and behavior control the future does not look bright. The way that some of these kids learn to survive in the midst of emotional ups and downs is far from healthy. Some of them isolate in order to avoid the emotional challenges of life, and others may turn to drugs and alcohol. Some kids ultimately act out their anguish violently.

Instead of delving into whatever made Nancy into a smothering mother let's look at what can really be done to help in a situation like this.

Day 5 in the play group.

There is a new game going on in the circle of infants. It is so much fun that even Bob is straining towards the kids from his mother's lap. Nancy moves herself closer to the inner circle so that Bob doesn't tear the blouse that she is wearing. Then Bob makes his move away from her and she is close enough that both of them feel OK. Bob looks back at her. She looks away. He starts to approach her looking worried but then she smiles and says "You can play, Bobbie. It's alright."

Little Bob seems to consider this and turns towards the other kids. His mother backs out of the circle. In just a few minutes Bob looks back and sees her at a distance. Then he rushes back to her lap.

It's just a small step for this baby but it is an important one. When Nancy lets her child guide the action both of them are more secure. She let him go and let him come back when he wanted to. Now she is repairing bond between them. They are rebuilding this important step.

Nancy as we can imagine, had her own hard time when she was a baby. We can see it in how she interacts with little Bob. It is often useful for parents to evaluate their own attachment patterns so that they can help their infants.

Parent Attachment Evaluation

Please answer	yes	no
1. I get close to people easily		
2. I like to be around people		
3. I can say what I think and feel around others		
4. I feel anxious or sad when I am alone		
5. I am basically a loner		
6. There are one or two people who really make me feel happy or sad. They know what buttons to push.		
7. I can lose a friend and not suffer over it.		
8. I like to be affectionate		
9. People tell me I am controlling		
10. I can let people be themselves		
11. My family likes to get together just for the fun of it.		
12. I keep in contact with my close friends for a long time		
13. I have an "ideal" view of the person who will be right for me and I haven't met him or her yet.		
14. I can be intimate and I enjoy it		
15. I know what love feels like and it is a good feeling		
16. I definitely have fond memories of my dad or my mom or grand-parent.		
17. Love is just another 4 letter word		
18. I fantasize about living far away from everyone.		

For parents who answered yes to questions 4, 5, 6, 7, 9 and 13, 17, 18. You, yes you, may have an attachment problem or disorder. This may amaze you because for years you have functioned around this problem. Around is the key word here because when you have difficulties beginning, or maintaining or ending a relationship there is pain involved. The pain relates to not feeling loved or not having trust and support. So you learned to deal with the pain. But now we know that your attachment style will impact the way you relate to your baby and the way that your baby develops self control. It is time to look forward and take some risks so that you can *reach and teach* your child. If you can't bond warmly and completely with your baby, the task of teaching self control is very hard.

We suggest that parents do some research into books that help with issues of intimacy, relationships, etc.

It is now time to ensure that your baby knows that his *"teacher"* is trustworthy, consistent and supportive.

Infant Attachment Evaluation

Please answer	yes	no
1. My baby likes to cuddle in my arms		
2. My baby goes easily with strangers.		
3. My baby cries when I move out of sight		
4. My baby doesn't like when I pick him up		
5. My baby reaches his arms up to me		
6. My baby likes it when I put my face near hers		
7. My baby follows me with his eyes when I move around him		
8. My baby calms down when I hold her		
9. My baby cries or struggles when I hold her for awhile		
10. My baby plays with my hair and face		
11. My baby seems disturbed (pushing me away, crying loudly,) when I come back after a few hours and hold her.		
12. My baby frequently smiles at me.		
13.. My baby creeps around with enjoyment when I am near him		

Parents, if you answered yes to items 2, 4, 9, and 11, you will want to do the exercises that follow. It is more important that you now look ahead to repairing your bond with the baby than worry about how it happened. There are many, many causes of what is called attachment disorders; some begin with the infant and others with the parent. Some of the most effective methods of building a trusting and secure bond are described below. Please note that the goal is that the baby enjoy and then trust being in your presence while he or she is in a positive state. The goal is not to make the infant respond to you by pressure of any kind.

Infant-Parent Attachment Exercises

1. Time to bond; set aside 15 minutes at a time, during the day. Sit on the floor with your infant in a place where he or she can crawl safely. Provide a few bright and interesting toys (ball, doll, cup and spoon). Now for the hard part and that is for you to watch and admire what your baby does. The point of this exercise is to let the baby direct the action. You are going to respond to the infant, verbally, facially and behaviorally.

    Example: the baby sits there and looks around; parent softly comments on how "good" the infant is, how "good" it is to sit and be with her.

    Example: the baby crawls off and away. Try to entice her back; tap spoon on cup, laugh, and play with another toy that makes noise. If she doesn't come back on her own then go and gently get her and try again. If it doesn't work try again later on and keep at it without pressuring her. Make sure that the toys are one's that will attract her.

    Example: the baby starts to play with a toy by examining it, picking it up. Now's your chance to try to engage him in the game. Talk about what he is doing with the toy. Get down closer and put a finger on the object. Try to get his eye contact with you. Do this easily and without pressure. **Your goal is to get the baby to enjoy being in your company while he is having a positive experience.**

2   Early Soothing. It is useful to pick up the infant when he or she is distressed. The baby will learn to associate you with his comfort zone. This builds security and trust.

3.   Earlier Steps. Go back to the mirroring exercises. This is often a good way
to re-establish contact with infants and even older children.

Here is an interesting case from our work in the hospital.

Ben is an 11 year old boy who was brought in by his group home manager. He is getting into all kinds of arguments and fights with the other kids in this home for children with behavioral problems. On this particular day, the manager of the home didn't have time to get Ben over to his regular doctor. The situation looked very bad and Ben was threatening to hurt himself if he has to stay in his room for discipline.

In the interview room, Ben is slumped down in a large chair looking at his hands which are clenched in his lap. The routine questions are answered with a curt "yes" or "no".

"Can you look at me, Ben?" The interviewer says

He gives a quick glance and then his eyes are again focused on his hands.

"Is there a reason why you don't look at me?" The interviewer says wondering what kind of response she might get from this child. This is the uncertain point because kids can say anything and some of it can be pretty rude.

"Your eyes look like you been crying." Ben says.

"Crying?" The interviewer says. "Maybe it's my glasses. They're rosy tinted."

Interviewer takes off her glasses.

"Now tell me if I look like I've been crying." Says the interviewer.

Ben looks at her with a serious expression on her face that makes her smile. He looks like any other kid who hates to be interviewed and wants to go outside and play. His little face studies her for a minute and then a tiny smile appears on his face.

"How do you think I look now, Ben?"

"Good." He says and that response makes my smile widen. That's a compliment from an 11 year old!

Ben tries very hard not to grin but I'm smiling happily and he can't help himself. Then he asks if he can try on my glasses. When he does he looks so funny I laugh and he relaxes and laughs with me.

This may not be a big deal in terms of the kind of therapy that Ben needs but it is the beginning of my trying to find his comfort zone. When I get him relaxed and content we will form an emotional bond. Then I can begin to teach him how to read my expressions and most importantly, to trust me to find his comfort zone when he's bringing up sad or angry memories. He can explore the new environment of his emotions without acting out his feelings.

The Basic Rules of Attachment: S.P.C.

It is often helpful to have a basic model for what secure attachment relationships contain in general. Here they are.

Seeking: The person tries to stay close to the attachment figure. This is especially evident when the person is anxious, depressed or threatened. It can clearly be seen when the individual is exploring new territory.

Protest: The person tries to actively avoid separation from the attachment figure as in crying, verbalizing.

Continuity: The person stays emotionally attached even when the other person is not there. Substitutes for the attachment figure are not adequate and there is grieving, pining behavior when the attachment figure does not return.

Finally, there are certain "RED FLAG" symptoms of a disturbed attachment that every parent should look for and take seriously when they occur with babies or older children:

1. Indiscriminate affection with strangers

2. Not cuddly with parents or resisting closeness.

3. Constantly demanding

4. No eye contact

5. Constantly clinging

6. Chronic and severe sleeping, feeding or other disturbances when the child is medically healthy.

7. Developmental lags **may** indicate attachment problems; no babbling, no reaching out not responding to parent voices. First, of course the infant's medical condition must be assessed (hearing, vision, coordination)

This has been an exhausting chapter. Many parents have had less than perfect experiences with their own parents during early childhood. The subject of attachment and bonding may bring up some memories that are not pleasant. There is never an ideal time to deal with your own attachment history but now is a good time to begin. Your attachment style will have a great impact upon your child in the important area of self-control as we have demonstrated. We know that creating a relationship that is secure and yet allows the "other" to feel independent and free is one of the most difficult things to do. But we must try to do it for the infant's sake.

You will move up from this Step with a perspective on attachment that will help your child move rapidly in the direction of self control and then emotional intelligence.

"I am close by." This is a statement that comes from the heart. It comes from the heart of self control because that feeling of security empowers children and adults to remain in their comfort zone while learning new things. Self control is not about shutting down the natural exploratory instincts in children. Self control is about exploration and seeking learning experiences within limits and those limits are defined by where the parent is at this stage of the game. Later on, this healthy physical and emotional exploration will be under the child's control and he or she will depend upon the guidelines set during this important step. It is sometimes difficult to find that balance between protecting the child and over protecting him. We suggest that you try the following:

1. Know the area that your child is exploring and take any necessary precautions.

2. Try to limit taking the child into areas where there is so much danger that you have to contain his activities.

3. Practice silent expressions of closeness; Stand attentively by the child or other person without calling attention to yourself. Let your body posture and face expressions communicate closeness.

4. Say the words "I am here for you." To your children when it is appropriate.

5. Be there when your child is actively exploring his environment whenever you can be available.

A Sneak Preview; Imagine your child 15 years from now. He is up on a bridge with several of his friends. They are all having fun testing their courage. One youngster is hanging over the rail. He yells to the others to do the same thing and several of them are trying to hang on by one hand. Your child weighs the risks and decides that hanging off of a bridge is dangerous and not at all fun. It just doesn't feel like he has anything to gain from risking his life. Not to that extent! When you think about it, part of what you taught him as a child was to explore safely and be able to get back to where you want to be. Back to that Comfort Zone! Now he is using this lesson and feeling pretty good about it.

Step Five: Sharing and Self Control

On a bright Sunday morning, Marla, Dan, and the kids are in the park enjoying the day. Marla watches Jill as she unpacks her little picnic basket full of toys, lining them up carefully. "That's nice, Jill." Marla says thinking about Jill's neatness and the fact that she left the house in a state of disarray. Ever since Mike learned to toddle around she's been taking delicate objects and putting them on high shelves. The house looks topsy-turvy but even that didn't stop Mike from pulling a lamp down as he struggled to stand up yesterday. He is 11 months old today.

Marla sighs and looks over at Dan and Mike. The toddler is lumbering off on an uneven course away from his father. He holds his arms out for balance and sometimes he will scoot down and crawl faster than he can walk. Now he's coming back towards Dan with a gleeful expression on his face. Dan's even more excited about his learning to walk and cheers his son on.

"He has so much energy!" Marla says to herself as she sees Mike tumble, get up and walk in another direction with Dan close behind.

"Look at him!" Dan yells as Mike heads towards her with an ear to ear grin and rosy cheeks.

The toddler steps onto the blanket and sees Jill's toys laid out in a colorful array. His eyes grow huge as he studies the toys. He squats down. His little hands reach out. He grabs one. Then he holds it up like a trophy for his mother to admire. Mike looks from the toy to his mother with an unspoken message. Marla sees a look on his face that touches her heart. "Yes" she says to herself. "I see the light in your eyes."

Jill says "Oh no!" and takes the toy sending Mike into a loud crying jag until Dan comes back and soothes him. It lasts only momentarily and then Mike wants to toddle off again with Dan in pursuit.

"He's a bad boy, Mom he takes my toys away." Jill complains.

"Mike's not bad, dear, he's just learning about things around him and he has a lot of energy." Marla says and feels her own stamina ebb away.

Mike like many toddlers is full of energy. It looks like there's no stopping him now that he can walk. And he sure does want to get up and go, go, go! Keeping an eye on him is pretty daunting. Walking is what most parents applaud at this exact stage. But as important as the baby's intense forward motion appears to be it is not the defining milestone of this step in terms of self control. When we look beyond locomotion and the other wonderful happenings of this stage we find another incredible sign that the baby is on track for developing self control. This sign is in the baby's efforts to pause and to **share his emotional experiences with others.**

The ying and yang of self control can be seen in the toddler's behavior at this point. In Mike's example, he sets himself off in forward motion, propelling himself towards something of interest. And then he pauses, he delays a moment so to speak, and focuses on something. In this brief time of delayed motion he becomes able to share his experience with another person. Even if it is just a toy it is so very important. **At this age, the self- control milestone is in the sharing of emotional experiences.**

What is new and important is his ability to share a special emotional experience with a special person; a person with whom he feels secure and understood and this is the adult who still is in control of his comfort zone.

Sharing of emotional experience is at the very core of self control and many believe that it **is the heart** of the capacity to control fluctuating emotions and behaviors well into the adult realm

Many of us as adults continue to lean on other people in a healthy way when we are trying to managing our feelings. This is especially useful if we are on a roller coaster of emotions and cannot find our comfort zones by ourselves. Even as adults, coping with anxiety and stress is difficult to do alone. Your friend, your partner and your close family members help you to reduce anxiety, to increase hopefulness and to get off the roller coaster. Sharing emotional experiences is important throughout our lives in order to stay balanced and in our *Comfort Zones*. We want our kids to develop this capacity so that they can use this resource naturally. We want them to be comfortable, social human beings. We know that they must control their feelings and actions in order to fit in, to have close relationships to learn things from others. This sharing is the heart of self in self control. It begins here and has been built on the steps that preceded this phase.

And now we present a case that demonstrates what a creative 5 year old does when she has no one to share with.

Melanie is a pretty, bright 5 year old who has been in day care since she was 3 months old. She has an active little mind but the day care center was full of kids just like her. When she's at home her mother is very, very busy trying to keep a roof over their heads. Mom herself is stressed and keeps her feelings to herself. She has had some bad experiences with telling people how she feels. The last person she expressed her true feelings to walked out on her and the baby.

Melanie has never really had sharing experiences with her mother. Their interaction is warm but Mom is problem-focused and likes to get things done. Melanie has learned, very quietly, to share things with her imaginary friend. She began with talking to her toy bear, but Mom didn't like that one bit. So now that she is older she can conjure up this friend anytime, anyplace and have a good time. In school her teacher accuses her of "day dreaming" and she tries not to do it a lot. But it feels so good to have someone who is near by and gets excited when she gets excited or gets sad when she gets sad. It's comforting to have some other entity who shares her unique emotional experiences. The other kids in school can go do whatever they want. She doesn't care because she feels pretty good by herself.

Many kids from age 3-5 have imaginary playmates and this is not a serious symptom unless, as in this case the child learns to use the playmate instead of other people. That is unless the child becomes isolated and doesn't climb the rest of the steps.

It is amazing and true that the toddler's brain is ready and able at this time to benefit from the sharing of emotional experiences. The nervous system of the toddler is now able to tolerate more intense levels of positive stimulation, and the brain is very sensitive at this time to the emotionally expressive face. The brain systems supporting memory, and cognitive areas have matured. The developing brain and the new behaviors go hand in hand. Although the toddler is very busy most of the time, a great deal of his activity is within range of the primary caretaker. A trustworthy adult is usually near by to protect and to share in the new experiences.

During this period it is important for parents and others to recognize where the milestone is in the toddler's development towards self control. It can often get lost or overlooked as parents try to protect their energetic babies, or teach them skills that seem to be important. What is most important at this time is whatever it is that your toddler finds emotionally rewarding and tries to share with you. He or she may actually point to the object of interest and then gaze at you for a response. The bird on the grass, or the leaf on the sidewalk or the hat on your head may be far more interesting than flash cards with A, B and C in bold red letters. When you encourage your toddler to share experiences you nurture the heart of self control. You bring the child one step closer to emotional intelligence!

Dan has a friend Geraldo who has a child the same age as Mike. This 11 month old toddler is able to nod his head "yes" or shake it "no" correctly when Geraldo holds up a number card and asks "Is this the number 8?" Geraldo is very proud of his son and spends a lot of time practicing the skill. What is actually important about their interaction is the sharing part of the activity. Little Ed gets a lot of time with his father if he goes along with the game and he's smart enough to play a lot in order to share this experience with Dad. Of course, Geraldo has chosen the activity of interest and not the child. When little Ed gets tired then his father gives him over to Mom. Is there a message here for the toddler?

Let us *fast forward* to Ed, Mike and another familiar face in preschool and see where the sharing comes into play in terms of self-control These kids are now 31/2 years old.

> *Mike is surrounded by sights and sounds that are intriguing. The girl next to him is in and out of her little chair, Ed, in back of him is jumping up and down singing and the smell of lunch time hamburgers is in the air. Wait a minute. The teacher holds something in her hands as she says something. He strains to hear her because she has paper and finger paint and he loves to paint pictures. Ed stops singing for a moment and then starts all over again.*
>
> *"Time for painting." Teacher says. . Mike watches her face and her movements as she puts the paper on a clean table. He catches her eye once or twice and he feels like they are doing this together. He goes over and stands with several other children who are excitedly pointing and gesturing as she explains what she's doing. He's heard the instructions before "We're going to do this together so stay at this table when you paint." He struggles to hold in his bubbling excitement until she counts to three on her*

upheld fingers. He holds his fingers up just like she does. "Ready one, two, three, paint". He watches her lips for the last word to come out and then he knows he can start painting. They're on the same page so to speak.

Cathy from playgroup is also in this class. You remember Cathy with the pacifier. She still uses it occasionally but not in school. Cathy doesn't like the smell of paint. When the teacher announces painting time she felt bad. Now teacher is paying all of her attention to the kids who were painting and Cathy isn't happy. There's no one to do anything special with. She's out of her comfort zone and can't get back. She knocks over another kid's tower of blocks. The kid yells and Cathy gets the teacher's full attention. Not a good solution to her problem but then she's only 3 1/2 years old. When the teacher talks to her and then engages her in another game she relaxes and feels better. A few minutes together, participating in a special task is what she needs. She's back on track.

Sharing emotional experiences doesn't always involve hugging, or words. We can see it happen when people tune into each other and control themselves as a result of understanding the other's messages.

When we go back to Mike in the park we can see that in this important stage we're not looking for perfect self-control. We don't expect toddlers to control their fluctuating emotions and know how to direct their behavior. They can't do that expertly until much later. What is important is that they can at around 10, 11 months pause and share emotional experiences with an involved adult. This will set the stage for what Mike and Cathy can do later on. Cathy was able to be comforted by her teacher, and helped to *manage her unhappy feelings with help* and then become engaged in another activity. There was a strong element of emotional sharing in what happened between

Cathy, Mike and the teacher. And it was this emotional sharing that helped them with the vital task of self-control.

And what about Bob and Brandon? We don't have to imagine what is happening now that they are toddlers.

> *At Mikes first birthday party all the play group kids are assembled with their mothers. Marla has converted the living room into a play area for the kids. She has balloons, party hats, small safe toys and paper horns on the living room table. All breakable objects are in closets. It's not clear if any of the toddlers understands that this is a birthday party but they are roaming around trying to figure out what's going on.*
>
> *Mike has his crown on his head but takes it off after Dan snaps a picture. Cathy holds a present in her arms and easily lets her mother take it and put it with the pile of gifts. Brandon goes over to where the gifts are. All the mothers take a long breath and hold it. He begins to pick the pretty packages up one at a time and then throw them to the floor. All mothers exhale as Barb says "No, bad boy" and puts the gifts back into a pile. Brandon grins and does the same thing. Barb says "No! No!" in a louder voice and picks him up carrying him screaming to the couch where she plops him down. He immediately scrambles off and she chases him as he runs wildly around the living room and kitchen.*
>
> *Bob has been sitting quietly with his mother holding onto a small gift. He grasps it tightly as Brandon runs around. His mother tries to take it but he holds on tighter. It's like his security blanket for the moment.*
>
> *"Let's play a game!" says Barb, holding onto*

Brandon's hand as he squirms away from her. She puts Brandon down on the carpet and sits next to him.

Cathy glances at her Mom and then sits down waiting for "the game" with an expectant look on her face Brandon's face is red but Mom has his hand and he sits with a frustrated expression on his face. Mike looks over at Marla and she signals him to sit down. He sits next to Cathy. Then Nancy sits down with Bob in her lap. He's still gripping the gift.

The "game" turns out to be way beyond the toddler's attention span and Dan takes over by stepping into the circle and pretending to be a variety of different animals.

"Bow wow" he says and Cathy laughs with delight. "Moo! Moo!" he says and the toddlers are having a good time. Brandon likes the noises and the excitement of this game and Bob is tuned in as well. When Dan gets tired and says, "That's it kids" Bob starts to cry and can't seem to stop.

After feeding the kids cake and ice cream Mike is told to open his gifts. Marla has prepared for this by getting each toddler a toy of their own. Brandon tears into his present and then tries to grab one from Mike who looks at Dan for help. Before he can intervene, Barb scoops up her child and heads for the door. As the party winds down Bob has dozed off in his mother's lap, and Cathy and Mike are playing with a new plastic truck. They are engrossed in rolling it around and Mike lets her do it most of the time. Cathy gets up to follow her mother when she goes to get their jackets.

There's nothing **bad** about any of these kid's behaviors. They're just toddlers who depend upon adults to get them back on track in terms of their emotions and behavior when the going gets rough. Parties are really tough with all the commotion and no time to really stop and share what is going on. It's like being lost in a crowd and some youngsters just don't do well with it.

When we look at the behavior of some of these toddlers we think that they may not be like this in the future. They're still "babies" and maybe they will grow out of some of their "babyish" behaviors. They will all learn to share and give easily and freely. Take Bob for example. He's certainly not going to be holding onto gifts at parties ten years from now, is he? Will Brandon be taking things that don't belong to him when he's a teenager at a social get-together? Which of these behaviors will go away and which will be a permanent part of the child's personality?

Although we cannot predict the outcome 100% we do know that the behaviors showing missed steps in developing self- control usually don't repair themselves on their own. We look with some concern at young children at this age who have consistent problems with participating in and enjoying simple social interactions that involve sharing. While we don't expect these babies to be able to cooperate on many levels we do hope that they will, in situations where their parents or caretakers are present, be able to begin to share the positive emotional flow.

Looking ahead, Baby Bob may grow up to be able to participate in social gatherings but there's a good possibility that he may remain anxious and insecure. Perhaps he'll just avoid the fun *and* the bad feelings. Little Brandon may not end up acting out in social situations but he may have some real problems getting into the shared "fun" aspect of the group. Perhaps he'll devise his own kind of amusements or find a group of people who also can't get involved on an emotional level.

Emotional habits are very hard to break. They are formed very early and become the model for our ways of coping with emotional experiences in the world.

Mike's sister Jill, for example, is a great at sharing and caring and she is way up there climbing the steps towards self control. And yet, sometimes even her strategies fall short of her goals and her expectations. Here is an example.

We know that Marla is very busy with Mike at this stage of the game. To Jill it seems as if she's the forgotten child and sometimes it gets frustrating. She is a bright little almost-4-year-old and she has learned how to say what she wants, how to be polite, wait her turn and help Mom with Mike. But today, it's simply not working because she wants to practice a ballet exercise and have Marla sit and watch her for as long as it takes to get it perfect. Jill likes things to be as perfect as possible. From her clothes to her hair and the projects that she does things just have to be...well perfect. Today Jill doesn't want to share her time and her mother with Mike!

On this particular day Marla has several things going on at the same time and she tells Jill to "be patient" just once too many times. Jill feels let down after she hears the words. She had expected that now her mother would give her the time. She doesn't want to play with her dolls again! She doesn't want to draw a silly picture of her ballet class again! She can't ask her mother the same question again!

On the roller coaster of her emotions, Jill can't find the strategy to get out of this emotional mess. Suddenly, she bursts into tears while Marla is feeding Mike.

"Throw him out the window!" She says, stamping her little feet. Then she sits down on the floor in a bundle of misery. Marla is in a quandary. Who wouldn't be?

Having two children on different Steps of the self-control ladder can be a real challenge. And many parents do have other kids. It is important at this time to leap ahead and make a few points about how to balance yourself in the midst of this kind of problem when you want both kids to achieve self-control. First, let's take a look at how Marla handles the situation.

> *Marla, somewhat shocked at Jill's statement, recognizes that her daughter is saying something that she needs to pay attention to. She wipes Mike's chin, puts the spoon down and says to Jill. "Yes, I know taking care of a baby is a lot of work. Instead of throwing him away maybe we can figure out how to give you some time. What do you think?"*
>
> *Jill looks up at her with wet eyes and doesn't say anything. Mom's words are running through her mind. Then she has an idea. "Stop feeding him and watch me!"*
>
> *Marla smiles as she gazes at the little, serious face below her and says. "How about we finish feeding and both of us watch you do the ballet?"*
>
> *Jill almost says "No. Do it now!" She knows that Mike's feeding can take a long time. She asks "How long to finish?"*
>
> *Marla looks at the bowl of food. Mike seems to be more interested in Jill's interaction with Mom than in eating.*
>
> *"Just a couple of minutes, Jill. Your brother seems to be more interested in you than the food anyway."*
>
> *At this statement Jill smiles and gets up. Her brother is watching her intently. She likes that serious look on his little face when it is directed towards her. She reaches for the spoon and helps Marla finish up. Then they all troop into the living room for the greatest performance of her life.*

What seems simple here is going to be an effort to put into practice.

That is because it involves parental self-control. In the middle of an emotional crisis, when you are being pulled in two equally important directions it is not easy to remember your own strategies for controlling the roller coaster of emotions and getting into your Comfort Zone.

Before we tackle this it is important to look back at Jill's behavior and the role that her "perfectionism" plays in her ability to manage the roller coaster of emotions. The need to be "perfect" can set a young child off on a difficult course because they tend to worry about things, demand a great deal of themselves and others and sometimes avoid doing things when they think it won't be perfect. The anxiety and the avoidance are not what parents are looking for in terms of healthy self-control. Many young children who strive for perfection are encouraged to do so and the problems show up later on. What causes this perfectionism is less important right now than how to deal with it so as to keep your child in her comfort zone and able to manage challenges without distress. At the end of this chapter is a strategy for helping the "perfect" child.

It may be very helpful at this point to review **your** strategies for managing the flood of feelings that can surge up at any time. And to remember that self control is all about finding that comfort zone inside so that we can think and direct our behavior appropriately. Self-control is not blind compliance, or shutting down our emotions.

A Quick Parental Review of Self Control Strategies

1. Remember that *you* are the adult. *You* have learned to share.

2. Model the attitude of calm attentiveness

3. Do your individual stress busting exercise; count to ten, visualize the positive, breathe deeply and let it out, see the situation in a humorous light.

4. Ask yourself "What is the problem?" "How serious is the problem?"

5. Test out a solution.

And now back to the kids.

Ways to Evaluate Your Child's Sharing Aptitude

Please pick a or b or c

My toddler   (a) likes to play with me in sight
                         (b) likes to play alone
                         (c) has no preference

My toddler   (a) looks at me when we play
                         (b) looks around when we play
                         (c) looks away when I gaze at him

My toddler   (a) points at things
                         (b) sometimes uses his hands to point
                         (c) never points

My toddler   (a) tries to get my attention all of the time
                         (b) can play alone some of the time
                         (c) needs me to encourage him to play

My toddler   (a) is difficult to console when he wants something he
                                can't have
                         (b) is easy to console
                         (c) is usually impossible to console.

My toddler   (a) gets excited when I get excited
                         (b) cries when I get excited
                         (c) ignores me when I get excited

My toddler likes to (a) toddle or crawl away from me and then come back.
                         (b) toddle away and keep going.
                         (c) stay right by my side.

My toddler   (a) shows excited delight when he discovers something
                         (b) cries with new experiences
                         (c) stays calm in new situations

In looking over this questionnaire it is important to remember that infants express themselves differently. Therefore some of the behaviors described above my not exactly describe what your child does.

Questions 2 ,3 ,6, 7, and 8 are of concern for this stage. Parents are aiming for the (a) type of behavior in their infant in those questions. If you need to move towards that goal the following exercises will help.

Exercises to Improve Sharing Skills

1. Have a special time and place for sharing experiences with the child. Do it when you and he are in a good mood. Watch and listen to the baby. Let him capture your attention. Let him guide the action with toys or other play materials and share the excitement, the wonder, verbally and with face expressions.

2. It may be a good time to get to know your growing toddler's comfort zones. They may well be different now. Make a new temperament chart; this chart is more detailed for the baby's growing abilities; such as his awake state, his emotional state when he eats, when he plays, when you dress him, when in a new situation, when he can't have something. Use this to find new comfort zones; such as he is happy when I go into him early in the morning to pick him up. Use this time for sharing experiences!!!!!!!

3. Look at family patterns of sharing emotional experiences. Do you share as a family? If not it may be time to start some special family togetherness projects.

Special Tools for the child who has to be perfect.

1. Some of these kids are very sensitive to over-stimulation. For example a child who strives for a gold star every day for homework may be so worried about not getting the star that she cannot focus. The trick here was to keep track of her progress without the stimulating gold star (try praising her progress verbally after three days) and ignoring unsuccessful days.

2. Some children are very sensitive to changes in routine because they strive for perfection. They may even explode when the routine is changed. The trick is to make changes slowly, to let the child help with the changes. For example if you need to change the dinner hour from 5pm to 6 pm you might help him make that shift by using 15 minutes of that time for doing something fun with the child. When he adjusts you may be able to reduce the amount of time or keep it if the two of you are enjoying it.

3. Look for and reward any evidence of flexibility in the child. Kids show

flexibility in very subtle ways; letting a sibling play with his toy, letting a parent help with a task, even correcting a simple mistake (wiping up a spill, taping together something that is torn.)
Milestone for the perfect child: He can adjust to small changes without anxiety.

The milestone for this step as a whole is that you and your baby can enjoy experiences together and the baby is beginning to get into the **shared joy** of the larger social group. It is usually a good idea to start with small social activities (like Mike's little party) and to be very near by. You are still the one to create a sense of security and to repair any catastrophes on the roller coaster of life. You are still the one who can help your child find his Comfort Zone.

You will move up from this Step with information that was once considered to be relatively unimportant in the development of the child. *Now we know* that sharing is part of the process of developing self control and plays an enormous role in emotional intelligence. Children and adults who enjoy sharing emotional experiences are motivated to control their emotions and behavior. Impulsive acting out for attention is not usually condoned in our society. Therefore showing children how to positively share important experiences will help to motivate them to control their impulses and remain part of the social group.

Raising a child with good self control skills means a great deal of sharing your *self* with that small person. Whether you are perfect or less than perfect in your own estimation, your child wants to share your world of experiences. And he will share his world with you. Your goal is for the child to enjoy the sharing experience so that he will learn the rest of the self-control skills. Therefore we suggest that you do the following:

1. Let your hair down, take off those fragile glasses and loosen that belt.

2. Get down where your child is

3. Share a few happy and care free minutes with your youngster.

4. Let your child guide the action and show you where the fun is!

A Sneak Preview; Imagine your child 12 years from now. It is an important day in his life and he is as confused as he can possibly be. Your youngster tried drugs for the first time and he feels as though you, his parent may reject and hate him. He is on an emotional roller coaster and he doesn't know how to get off. Deep down he wants to be part of your life and the family's life. He knows he can't survive without you and he doesn't want to loose his family. After a few days of misery he asks for you to listen to what he has to say and you do listen. He is sharing an experience with you and counting on you to be there for him. This ability to share and to risk opening up emotionally is what you taught him many years ago. Now he depends upon that early lesson. If you think about it, he is doing exactly what you want him to do and if you keep that door open he will come to you again for help and guidance with life's challenges.

Step Six: Words and Self-Control

As Dan opens the front door on a cold, dark evening the aroma of dinner greets him. It is late on a Wednesday evening. He's exhausted after having put in an extra 3 hours on an important project and all that he wants to do is to sit down, eat something and then close his eyes.

He closes the door softly behind him, in case Mike is already in bed. It's already 8: pm.

"Is that you, Dan?" Marla calls out from the bathroom where he can hear splashing sounds.

"It's me. I can get myself something to eat. You finish what you're doing."

Dan takes a plate of meatloaf and mashed potatoes to the table and sits down heavily. He's so worn out that even the delicious meal has little appeal. His thoughts go back to work where the bosses were in some kind of a high level meeting that had to do with the company budget.

As Dan's eyes droop he feels a tug on his jacket sleeve.

"Da?" The little voice says. Dan looks down and sees Mike in his brightly colored pajamas.

"Huh?" says Dan trying to focus his eyes.

"Weed?" says Mike looking up at him expectantly.

"Oh." Dan answers, rubbing his tired eyes. He knows what Mike wants. He wants Dad to read him a book before he goes to sleep.

"Weed?" Mike says again more insistently. His eyes are shining and his little mouth is open as if he has more to say. Mike's fingers are holding on hard to his father's jacket.

"OK," Dan mumbles getting up and taking

his hand. Let's go and read a book. In the living room Dan pulls a book off of the shelf and sits down on the couch. He opens the book but Mike stands there shaking his head no. The couch is so soft and Dan is so weary that he doesn't respond right away.

Mike's face flushes and his smooth forehead furrows. He's on the edge of something important. "Weed Bic Boopie." He says clearly.

Dan is caught for a moment trying to understand what book Mike wants. Now he has a problem. He is tired and wants to get some rest but Mike wants him to go through all the trouble of searching through the dozens of books until he finds the Bic Boopie whatever that is. One look at Mike's intent little face as he gazes up at him guides Dan to a decision. He gets down on the floor with all the books and one by one reads out the titles until they find The Big Bumble Bee. Mike holds it up like a trophy above his head and sits in Dan's lap while he reads all about the busy insect.

If we could get inside Mike's brain we would find that his father did something that was truly brain nurturing on several levels. When we look specifically at the domain of self-control the most obvious thing that Dan did here was to help Mike get into his comfort zone after a long delay. Waiting for Dad was a long delay for Mike. But there is so much more. When Dan stopped, listened and then responded to Mike's **words** the way that he did, he taught his child that words are powerful forces. Dan helped Mike to connect words with their meaning and with action that produced something positive. This connection will be learned by Mike and used when he has to manage a situation that is causing him discomfort. Language is connected in this way to self-control.

Many volumes have been written about the importance of language and its development during the childhood years. Far less attention has been paid to the role that language plays in the development of self-control.

What is in a word or two words that adds to a child's ability to manage the roller coaster of feelings and to direct his behavior? For a young child, words do more than signal what he wants or needs. Language goes beyond these basic things and becomes the means of communicating ideas and emotions. When ideas and feelings are *expressed* and then *received* by the parent, the child begins to understand what words really mean and what words can do. This understanding will help him to say what is on his mind, in his heart and remain within a workable comfort zone.

From the first words to the unfolding of entire sentences it will be the parent who interprets and who guides the child to the full meaning of words. They do this by receiving what the child says and demonstrating that what he says has significance.

This is a brain-building event. Parents have the unique opportunity by listening and responding, to help the child learn the significance of words, and the power of language to help us with stressful situations.

Communication that clearly expresses ideas and feelings and that is well received by someone who gets what we mean, is an incredible source of self-control. The receiving part is as vital as the expressing part as most adults know from experiences where we talk about something important to us and the other party just doesn't get it. Or when they misinterpret what we say and make us angry, frustrated or sad.

For young children, it is the first the parents who try to understand and to respond appropriately to what the child is trying to say.

In the anecdote above, Dan had a difficult decision to make. He could have given into his exhaustion (who could blame him) and read another book after trying to explain to a very young child just how tired he really was. But Dan read the meaning in Mike's plea for *Bic Boopie* and he took these words very seriously. In that moment he taught his son that words have significance, and that they lead to positive action. Words become important to the child in his efforts to get *beyond the roller coaster of emotions* and then solve the problem.

The early development of language is more than we can cover in this book. It is fact that infants tune into the human voice more than other sounds and that parts of the language system are inborn. By the age of 4 months, for example, babies may laugh in response to adult speech! At 7 months infants grasp the rhythm of sentences and they can tell when a sentence starts and stops. But, as with other capacities that we have seen unfold; the role of parental teaching is primary in terms of the full development of language. Speech develops explosively from the age of 12 months on with growth in all areas of language; receptive vocabulary, sentence production, grammar etc. From the first words parents must help the child connect language to meaning and to self-control.

When these connections are not made there are many kinds of things that may occur. The child will usually find some other way to express feelings and ideas and to get through the roller coaster of situations that confronts him. In some cases, such as that of Jane, the final result is inner discomfort.

Jane was raised in a large family. She was the 6th girl out of 7 siblings. The family was healthy in many ways and the children were taken care of by their parents, with help from grandmother and the older siblings. Jane had her toys and such but she was treated like the baby of the family and not taken very seriously. Jane learned that when she cried or gestured with her hands she usually got what she wanted or needed faster and easier than any other way. Everybody was just so busy that no one really sat down and listened to her or conversed with her in any consistent way. Jane's oldest sister was basically in charge of her and as a teenager she often disregarded what Jane was trying to say or gave her something to calm her down. For example, when Jane said "pay" which was her word for play, the sister would usually respond "Later. Go and find grandma." Then grandma would say "Go outside and play." Jane would

get frustrated, cry and be given a cookie or be told to "Be quiet."

In this way no one really responded to Jane's words and their true meaning which was, of course, "*Play with me.*" This happened every day while she was growing up.

Now, this is a very little thing. However when Jane grew up she found that she expected people not to respond to the meaning of her words in the way that she wanted. She had no belief in the power of her words or in the ability of other people to understand them. It made her very uncomfortable and stressed in social situations. Jane was simply not sure that her words would achieve what she wanted or needed. As she got older this problem developed into serious anxiety when she was around people. There was no way for her to feel comfortable except when she was by herself.

Children's first words are important messages about themselves and their world. If these messages are discounted, disregarded or responded to inappropriately the child has a difficult time using language to manage feelings and express ideas.

When children do not learn how to express themselves in meaningful language, a stressful situation can lead quickly to more *violent* loss of self-control. Some kids learn to express themselves in behavior that is aggressive, self-destructive and disruptive when they are faced with a hard task or a new situation. Their aggressive behavior acts to signal that the child is stressed and on the roller coaster but it also helps the *child avoid the task or situation that caused the roller coaster ride to begin.* In this way, the problem behaviors become more ingrained as unhealthy self-control strategies. The escape from the stressful task or situation is a reward for the problem behavior. This is a terribly vicious cycle.

Marla and Dan have a neighbor who demonstrates one of the other ways that adults who mean well can disrupt the process of language development. Whenever neighbor Gloria sees little Mike she hugs and kisses him. When he started with a few words she would swoop him up and talk and talk about how wonderful he was. Mike doesn't say one word now when she is around. There is no reason for him to even try to communicate with this loving woman. His words are as important to Gloria as the cute sounds that a pet cat makes. Mikes silent withdrawal helps him stay in his comfort zone when Gloria is around. If this kind of thing happened on a very regular basis he might find that words are a problem in themselves.

The early milestone in language development is in the child's expressing the meaning of the word to an adult who shows that he or she *gets it*. This process can be underway as early as 12 months.

Children develop very differently in their language abilities over the first three years. In very general terns, parents can get a sense of where the child "should be" in language development by following the following guidelines.

From 8 to 12 months many children understand several single words and look at objects that the parent looks at. They also are responding to the tone of parent's speech (harsh or soft) and this carries a meaning for them.

From 12 to 18 months children understand single words that are not in a routine scenario and let parents know that they note the object by using it.

From 18 to 24 months children understand the word for the object when the object is missing! They can locate missing objects when asked to do so.

From 24 to 36 months children understand three word sentences and can supply missing *information about objects* when asked.

Helping your child with language skills

1. Take the time when the child is trying to say something to stop, listen and respond in a meaningful way.

2. Use simple language when you talk with the child. Use consistent names for things and for feelings.

3. Make words interactive. When you read to the child, or tell stories, ask simple questions about what you are saying. Encourage comments from the youngster.

4. Notice how you and your partner talk together. Do you understand the meaning behind the words?

5. Watch the *tone* of your voice. Young children pay a great deal of attention to the tone as well as the words.

Help for parents whose children express themselves in behavior and not words.

What is easy for a parent may well look very hard for a child. Many children **can't tell you that a task is too difficult.**

For kids who may be stressed by difficult tasks;

Start with easy tasks. Make tasks simple. Not putting all toys away, just one or two. Use **verbal praise;** simple words for completing tasks and look at the child directly.

Watch for attention seeking behavior that is *not* related to the difficulty of the task; Give the child more alone time, routinely reward all positive behaviors.

Use language more in everyday situations. Use *narrative* to engage your child's attention:

1. Tell simple stories about when you were a baby: *Once upon a time when Mom was a baby she wanted to paint the house. The whole house from top to bottom What a job that would be! Her Mom said that's too hard so let's paint a picture.*

2. Make up simple, funny sayings about routine things: *Eating is a funny thing, when I eat I want to sing. Washing faces is so nice, now I think I'll do it twice.*

Using words to say what we mean and to keep us in our Comfort Zones can be difficult for people at any age. Have you said something recently and then stopped to reflect on the meaning of your words or the tone of your voice?

"I'm busy"

Translations: I don't care. Leave me alone. I am overwhelmed.

"I am tired"
Translations: Leave me alone. I am also sad or angry. I am
 bored.

"I am OK."
Translations: Don't ask me. I am just hanging in there. I don't
know what to say. I haven't decided how I feel.

"That's nice"
Translations: I have to say something. I have no real opinion
 about it but I don't want to hurt your feelings.

Parents are always making these statements and might want to
consider how a 12 month old child understands them. Having a child
gives us the opportunity to reflect on what we say and how it sounds
and what it all means. Language can empower or disable us as human
beings. Most of us tend to take it for granted that what we say is what
others understand. When a young child looks into your face and listens
to your tone of voice and your words it sheds a new light on what
language is and how it is used.

You move up from this Step with a new view on language as it
relates directly to self control and emotional intelligence! "I hear you!"
This is what adults say to each other. Many times we're left wondering
if the person actually "understood" what we said. They may be on the
phone or on the internet and we are left with a vague hope that they
do know what we mean. That vagueness and ambiguity can lead to a
lot of emotional distress and to mistakes in behavior.

It is important to really show a child that you have captured the
emotional meaning of their words if your goal is for the child to express
himself and understand other people's use of language. We hope that
you:

1. Spend the time and actively listen to your child's babbling.

2. Let the child know by your face and body language that you
   are listening to him.

3. Actively respond to your child's words by asking questions, repeating what he is saying and expressing positive emotional signs.

A Sneak Preview; Imagine your child 8 years from now. She is, unfortunately, caught up in a sad situation. One of her close friends has cancer and your child is very, very emotionally distressed. She is not in her Comfort Zone for many hours of every day as she rides a very steep roller coaster into the depths of despair. And yet she is going to school, doing her homework and behaving herself. Inside of her the tension is building up. One day she writes you a little poem and in it she clearly expresses her feelings. She uses words to convey her sadness and her fears of death. She uses language in a way that is comfortable for her. You taught her to do that. You let her know that when she spoke or wrote about her feelings that you would take her seriously. And so she did and now you can respond to her with love and comfort.

Step Seven: Empathy and Self Control

On a cloudy Saturday afternoon Dan and Geraldo are taking the boys to a little league game. Geraldo's 11 year old son, Bret plays for the Grey Whales and this is an important game for him. Before going to the park they grabbed a bite to eat at a spot that had a kid's playground right on the premises. Mike and Ed toddled over to the swings and Brent went with them. Dan thought that Geraldo looked edgy.

"How's it going?" he asked his friend as they ate.

"Ok, I guess." Geraldo mumbled and put down his burger. "I just can't stand being home too much. You know? The usual stuff. Pressures and things."

Dan waited for more but Geraldo stared off into space. He remembered that Marla had mentioned something about marital problems between the couple.

"Anything I can do to help?" Dan said sincerely.

"Nope. I just got to be strong and get through this." Geraldo said. "I have no time to get aggravated about it. With all the terrorism and stuff happening around us we just have to tough out the little problems. I want Ed to be strong and stand on his own two feet!"

Dan could see that his friend was unhappy but didn't want to open up. Geraldo threw his food away and called for the boys.

They arrived at the playing field and took seats close and up front so that Geraldo could cheer Brent on. The 11 year old was excited and anxious. He kept tying and re-tying his laces.

"Cut that out, son" Geraldo said curtly. "Go and win for me."

Brent ran off and Mike sat down next to Ed in between the two adults. Ed looked like his father, with tightly curled black hair and large expressive eyes. He was very focused on watching his big brother as the game began.

In the stands the cheering and yelling began. Mike was able to see the action and he cheered when Dan cheered. From time to time Dan held him up so that he could see even better. Mike was loving it.

Suddenly, one of the players fell and Brent catapulted over him slamming his face into the dirt. A hush fell over the crowd. Brent got to his knees and looked dazed. Someone in the crowd yelled "He's hurt get a doctor!"

Geraldo was on his feet and so was little Ed. Dan heard Geraldo blurt out "Damn!" At that moment Mike began to cry. He tugged at Dan's shirt with tears running down his face. Dan held him and tried to comfort him. "See, Mike, Brent is standing up now and he's going to be OK."

"He better wash that muck off and get back to the game." Geraldo said.

"Yeah. Back to game." Echoed little Ed. He had remained calm during the entire event and seemed content to sit and watch the rest of the game. Mike on the other hand had stopped crying but had lost interest. He whispered in Dan's ear. "Brent fell down." This seemed to linger in his mind. He told his mother about the fall when they got back home and she listened carefully. "You fell last week and hurt your knee, right,

Mike?" she said. He looked at his knee, then at his mother and smiled. "Bandage on it." He said softly.

There has been a great deal written on the subject of empathy; the ability to sympathize with another person's situation and feelings, to feel emotions similar to the pain or the joy of another human being. The key word here is *similar* because the inner emotions *are not exactly the same but come close enough to what the other person is experiencing.*

There has been a lot less written on when empathy develops and how it is connected to self- control. From what we know now, empathy develops as early as 16 or 17 months and it is an important part of the capacity to control emotions and behavior.

As we have emphasized earlier, self- control does not mean the imprisonment of feeling nor does it only relate to positive emotions. Control means the ability to understand, read, and share emotional expressions so that we can respond appropriately. That means using our intelligent minds and not being overwhelmed by fluctuating emotions.

In order to harness and manage our emotions, we first need to recognize what these feelings are. In earlier steps we talked about the infant's learning to identify and read emotional expressions from voice, face and body language. The reading or identifying of expressions was only part of the formula. In order to fully comprehend our feelings and those of others we need to know what these feelings are. We have to feel something similar. When a child recognizes pain in the face of another person, and he experiences something similar to that pain he has made a leap towards fully understanding the meaning of emotions. And this accurate reading and similar feeling is empathy. Empathy enables the child to understand the meaning of emotions as they apply to others and to him. With this understanding the child is better able for the most part to cope with the emotions of people, with emotional situations and with his inner emotional world.

In our example above, Mike demonstrated the *power of empathy*. He read the expression of pain on Brent's face, and heard the alarm bells in people's voices. Somehow he felt a similar bad feeling and it made him cry. In this way he expressed the feeling that could have bottled up inside him. And it was the feeling that most of the people around him felt because Brent had been hurt. When he cried, Mike's expressed emotions prompted his father to soothe him. In that way Mike achieved an emotional goal. He was helped to return to a comfort zone.

In our steps so far we have watched the milestones of self control appear and they have been guided and directed by the parents. Empathy becomes an internal moral compass. Its appearance marks the point at which the child understands and *begins* to try and manage his emotions and his behavior. And begin is the key word for once again, this capacity is continuing to unfold. The internalization of self control is what we are striving for in our 10 Steps. This Step is an important pre requisite.

Mike cried when Brent got hurt. This was not a loss of self-control as Geraldo might think, but the capacity to read and understand the emotional situation and respond appropriately for his age. Later on, he may not sob when a friend is injured but that pain that he feels will alert him and will help direct his behavior. Self- control is not about keeping a stiff upper lip when others are in trouble. It is about recognizing what they are feeling and deciding what to do. It is also not about hiding one's own feelings. It is about expressing them.

Little Ed didn't cry when his big brother slammed his face into the dirt. Even though Mike cried Ed either held his tears in or did not read the situation as a painful one for his brother. What might he do later on when a friend is hurt? If he doesn't feel some similar pain will Ed respond appropriately? Maybe he will ignore his friend, or laugh it off or get angry with the friend for getting hurt.

We have to assume that Ed missed one or more of the first steps towards self control. It would be hard for a child who has not learned the lessons of the 5 preceding steps to develop empathy. Empathy developed from the sharing of emotional experiences, the attachment to a trustworthy adult, the early reading of faces and voices and the parents understanding of the baby's earliest temperaments.

The way in which empathy helps us manage our feelings and direct our behavior can also be seen at the adult level. And so we leave the playground and enter Geraldo's home situation.

After the game Geraldo takes Ed home and his wife Anna asks how things went.

"Terrible." Geraldo says. "We lost the game. Brent made a fool of himself."

"Brent fell!" Ed adds looking up at his mother. She reaches out for Geraldo's arm as he leaves the kitchen. Alarm is written all over her face. Geraldo brushes her hand away and says. "He's fine! Just a couple of scrapes. The kid needs more practice and less piano lessons."

"More!" States Ed with conviction and picks up his own ball and bat.

Just then Brent comes in, covered with dirt and looking miserable. Geraldo stomps out of the room as the 11 year old hangs his head. There is silence as Ana struggles not to hold her older son. She wants to but Geraldo would be very angry if she "coddled" him at this point. And Brent might cry if she reached out to him. His father would hate to see tears on his older son's face. Brent looks at her and then goes to his room followed by Ed who brings his ball and bat with him. "Play more." He says as Brent closes the door to his room and throws himself on the bed.

And what's up with Geraldo? Clearly the connection between reading emotional expressions and feeling something similar was out of whack. Somehow his own feelings at seeing his son in pain and humiliated were translated into anger and betrayal. Perhaps he could read his son's emotional expression and then felt something else inside? Whatever it was, the results were that he became angry with his son. Lack of empathy led to the anger and the behavior that was not healthy for anyone at home.

To be in good control of one's emotions and behavior does not mean that one doesn't feel anxiety, anger, depression or guilt. It does not mean that one does not express these emotions. Negative emotions are signals for us that something is not quite right. They are red flags and sirens depending upon the intensity of the emotion. When Ed was an infant it was perfectly appropriate for Geraldo to protect him from the sirens and the wildly waving emotional red flags. His brain wasn't ready for the intensity of these signals. As a baby he couldn't have processed the emotional data or understood what it meant.

At 17 months most toddlers have seen, heard, and felt the emotions of anger, sadness and anxiety. In our society, the television, radio, computer and people are demonstrating all of these emotions. The toddler's brain and nervous system are now better able (in biological ways) to use some of this information. Without going deeply into the brain structures of memory and cognition that support the new learning it is important to know that again, brain growth and behavior go hand in hand. For some toddlers, the ability to feel similar feelings may be delayed for biological reasons. But many toddlers by the age of 18 months demonstrate that they do understand other's feelings, that they feel similar feelings and they also tend to try to comfort the one who is in pain.

The way that a young child expresses "similar feelings" (empathy) may strike adults as strange indeed. Parents have to understand their toddlers face, voice and body expressions pretty well in order to grasp the often unique ways in which the child shows that he has empathy.

We remember Cathy from preschool. She is a very active toddler who now seems to enjoy new experiences with relish. The pacifier has been left in a drawer and this child likes new and challenging opportunities. One day, however, she resisted going to the playground. Her mother was puzzled. Cathy cried when they arrived at the swings. Her mother looked at her in alarm. "What in the world was this all about?" Then she remembered something. It was a small thing, almost forgotten with all of the things that had occurred the last time they were there.

On that day, a boy had climbed on the swing and his older sister pushed him with such force that he fell off. He was stunned at first and they screamed and screamed. Cathy had been on the little slide at the time. All of the adults had gone to help the little boy and Cathy had stood near her mother completely silent. The event had not gone over her head, however. The fear in the little boy's screams had indeed touched her and she now wanted to avoid the scene of the disaster. Cathy had indeed felt a similar feeling. In the midst of the crisis, her expression had to be overlooked and could have forever gone unnoticed. Now her mother remembers that she was pale and unusually silent on the trip home that day. Now her mother recalls that Cathy woke up several times that night. And now she sees that her child has empathy.

Very active and very quiet children express feelings in different ways. Often their responses are mistaken for something else or are delayed for awhile. Parents need to know their child's expressions and have a good memory for recent events. The toddler's memory for significant events is also growing.

Little Ed sits outside of his brother's closed door for awhile and then goes outside. His mother watches from the window as he looks for something to play with. The family dog ambles over to see what's happening. Ed throws the ball for the old dog who doesn't want to play. Ed's face tightens. He throws the ball again and again, towards the old dog finally striking the dog on its side. Ed walks over and stands above the dog for a minute. Some fleeting emotion passes over his face and he bends down and pats the dog on the head. The dog looks up at him adoringly. Then he comes back into the house. The dog gets up and wanders off. Ed's mother tries to say something to him but he runs into the living room and turns on the TV. Whatever he's watching is making him laugh and his mother relaxes a bit thinking that he's over whatever was "eating at him." Hopefully, she thinks to herself, he will forget about it and move on.

The fleeting emotion that Anna saw in Ed's face may have been empathy. Young children can feel empathy even though they act as though they have not one drop of this important elixir flowing through their veins. Anna, as a mother, has been able to build this strength in her child and Geraldo, as tough as he is, actually expresses empathy at times. Little Ed does have this capacity and it will be very, very vital for his mother and others to support this strength whenever it appears. Sometimes parents have to look pretty hard to find the signs of empathy.

At this age, along with the capacity for empathy the ability to feel shame is developing. These emotions *can* work together to increase self control. Shame is a feeling that alerts us that we have not lived up to some expectation or standard. It is one of the signal emotions that makes us stop and consider what we are doing and perhaps change our direction. In terms of self control, shame can make us evaluate the situation differently. This important feeling is the one that makes us redden, want to hide under the table, and in general makes us very aware that we have done something that causes others to look at us in disgust. When a person understands the emotions of others he is likely to feel shame when he has crossed some line.

Shame can also trip a child as he climbs the steps to self-control. Parents and others who teach the child to feel ashamed on a regular basis may find that their youngsters are anxious or depressed. Self-control, as we know is not about punishment or about getting total compliance from a child or an adult. You can get this kind of subservience when you induce shame but this is not healthy self- control.

Marla and Jill are discussing the fact that Jill wants to go to a friend's house to play a new game. Marla is trying to explain to the little girl that she simply can't go until tomorrow. Jill is not happy. She controls her negative feelings and then she tells Marla that she is "Not a GOOD MOM today".

Marla looks into her daughter's eyes and tells her that these words are not very nice. She asks Jill to think it over. Jill ducks her head and a flush spreads across her face. She reaches up and hugs her mother. "Sorry." That is all that she has to say. Marla hugs her back and the child learns that she can make things OK and be forgiven.

In the toddler world, what counts most is what his behavior looks like in the eyes of trusted adults. Shame is experienced when the adult makes it clear that the toddler has done something that disgusts them. Shame can propel the child to try to correct the behavior so as to get the approval of the adult and thereby feel the positive glow of being good again. The fact that repairs can be successfully made gives the child an increased sense of security about expressing himself and trying new things.

When shame exists and continues without the *empathic response of an adult* then it is not useful for managing one's emotions and behavior. At this particular time in the toddler's life there are many opportunities for him to stumble, to make mistakes, to mess up what he is doing. There are also many opportunities for caring adults to let him know just how badly he's messed up. It is therefore very important that parents and others balance shame with empathy for the toddler's mishaps and mistakes. Shame without empathy is a deep, dark hole that can cripple the life of any child. It does not lead to self-control.

During dinner, Brent sits limply at the table while his father talks about the game. His cheeks redden when his father describes his "clumsy fall". Little Ed listens and watches Brent's ego deflate like a leaking balloon. Then Ed spills his milk and starts to cry. It's been a long, hard day. Geraldo tells him to stop "being a baby." Ed gulps down his sobs and leaves the table.

Later on his mother finds him lying on the couch sleeping. She sits next to him stroking his hair and wiping the tears from his cheeks. "He still looks like a baby" she thinks to herself.

There are studies showing that continued shame experiences without empathy on the part of caregiver can result in the child having overwhelming rage. An angry child who cannot understand his own or others feelings can be a time bomb in any situation. We see examples of this every day in our practice and the problem becomes explosive in the teen years. At this age, anger without empathy can and will destroy people's lives. Habits are hard to change and it takes a great deal of work to change the emotional habits of teenagers.

Here is a dramatic case from our work in the hospital:

Dan is a 15 year old who was brought into the emergency room by the police. He was a thin, tall boy whose arms were held tightly behind him by the handcuffs. Dan sat in a chair staring at the floor. One of the officers explained what was going on:

"We got a call from the school. They said that a kid was threatening to blow people away and he had a gun in his locker. When we got there several kids described Dan and we found him in the library. We took him to his locker and he opened it. He had a gun wrapped up in some gym clothes. That's why he's here. He says he wasn't going to use the gun but it was loaded."

Dan won't look at us when we ask him questions. His hair hangs over his face and he slumps in the chair. One officer shows us a note that he had in his pocket and it reads:

"If I die it's ok. But before I am shot I will take a few people with me. You know who you are and if you survive today I will hunt you into the next world. You can't torture me anymore. You can't call me fag and kick me in the butt and take my money. I was waiting for this time to come. Now the game is over and if just one or two of you die then I won this round."

What came to light later on was that Dan had been bullied most of his life. At home his parents and his older brothers pushed him around. He had been a small child, afraid of the dark and a bed wetter until the age of 11. **He was always ashamed of himself**. He had learned early on not to cry, and not to ask why no one cared to comfort him. In school he was always on the fringes, a loner who suffered verbal and physical assaults almost daily. Dan's shame was the strongest emotion he experienced until the anger took over. And then the rage was so deep and so painful that he just wanted to "get even". Even if he died trying.

Continued shame experiences can also lead to depression and anxiety as the child grows up. It is therefore up to the parent to ensure that the active, energetic toddler have opportunities to correct and to fix and to continue to enjoy his relationship with parents and the world.

For many adults, the subtle ways that a toddler expresses shame can easily be overlooked. The following examples can guide you as you interact with your child.

The subtle faces of toddler shame

1. looking away from the adult's angry or disappointed face

2. flushing when he or she is reprimanded

3. crying when he or she is reproached,

4. hiding the face behind hands or in parents clothes,

5. hyperactivity when criticized

The Empathy Evaluation for the Child

	Yes	No
1. When I read a sad story my child gets a sad expression on his face		
2. When I am expressing joy my child expresses joy with me		
3. When I am sad my child comes over to me and pats my face or body.		
4. When we (parents) are upset about something that is not child-related, my child questions it		
5. When we (parents) get angry at the child's sibling he comforts the sibling		
6. If someone gets hurt in preschool or daycare my child tries to tell me about it		
7. When an unfortunate event happens and the child knows about it he may have a hard time sleeping or eating.		
8. My child plays with dolls or action figures as though they have feelings.		
9. My child acts as though our pet has feelings just like he has.		
10. My child gets concerned (cries, asks questions) when someone has a physical injury; cut, red mark, etc.		
11. My child tends to want avoid a situation where there has been a tragedy; to the playground if someone fell off a swing, or to school if kids hit each other.		

If you rated the child 9 yes, or higher he or she is showing good empathy. It is still a good idea for you and especially parents who rated their children in the 3-7 range to do the exercises.

Empathy Exercises for your Child

1. Spend time positive reinforcing child's positive behavior, even the tiny stuff and decrease criticism

2. Empathy game with dolls; some children will get into this game. The mommy doll that goes to the hospital. Verbalize feelings about the mother and her child who is worried or scared.

3. The happy album. Start an album for happy family photos and drawings. Each day sit with child and add something or remember positive feelings that everyone shared.

4. Be an empathy role model. Talk about little things that are troubling you or the family in simple expressive terms. Not blaming such as Today was a hard day at work. I feel tired. What do you think I can do?

5. Take time to look and listen to your child's expressions of feeling (positive and negative) and share a similar experience of your own.

6. Use language; the toddler understands sad happy scared as words when paired with adult face and sound expressions; use them in your interactions with him and ask questions. Are you happy now?

We know that some kids need games that are more stimulating. There are ways to help the toddler who is sensation-seeking too:

1. Vary the above exercises daily.

2. Add activities with an element of surprise.

Here is one example: The face grab-bag game. Cut photos of happy or surprised or sad faces from magazines (or draw them) put in a bag and have him pull one and say what it is. Then both of you act out the emotion. Reward quickly with hugs and verbal praise.

In the scientific realm there is a huge focus now on the connection between lack of empathy and criminal behavior. Questions continue to pop up, especially after particularly bloody and senseless crimes:

"Can a person who abuses a child or an adult have empathy?"

"Can a person who repeats crimes such as assault have empathy?"

"Can you have empathy for animals and not people?"

"Can you have empathy for one group of people and not others?"

In the future, behavioral scientists may find hundreds of different kinds of empathy. We are interested in one kind and that form of empathy can be seen by parents as early as 17 months. It is expressed in the child's face, behavior and sometimes in words.

Before all of the scientific questions above find their answers we do know that the ability to empathize with another person's feelings is a vital part of self-control. It is part of the understanding of feelings within one's own self and empathy allows us to connect and communicate with others.

As parents grasp for ways to help the child control his behavior it is important that they use the shame technique with great care. Use it sparingly and always let the child know that you love him.

You move up from this Step with the latest information on Empathy and with the ability to help your child develop this wonderful capacity. Empathy is an empowering part of self-control because it enables us to understand and respond to other people in ways that are helpful and appropriate and not impulsive and destructive. Having empathy leads to more careful, thoughtful consideration of other people's situations and feelings. Life without any empathy is a lonely, frustrating and often dangerous experience as the lives of psychopaths show us very clearly. In order to eventually achieve emotional intelligence a child must be capable of reading other's emotional signals and then responding in healthy ways. We can see how empathy grows and flowers when the child feels not only comfortable and protected by the parent but also understood by the parent. And it is this deep level of emotional understanding between parent and child helps him to appreciate the feelings of others. Therefore, it may be useful to spend time and do the following:

1. Recognize the signs of empathy in people around you and in yourself

2. Actively support your child's empathic responses; verbal praise, hugging etc.

A Sneak Preview; Imagine your child 8 years from now. He's an active kid with a bit of a problem in math but doing relatively OK. This is the kind of average youngster who sails along not creating any problems and seeming to have a good time. Then one day you notice that he looks tired and a bit thin. You wonder why he is not eating as much and is tossing around in his bed so much that his sheets are in a tangle.

"Mom?" he says one morning. "How did it feel to die in the Twin Towers attack? It must have hurt something awful don't you think? I mean they were in a fire and couldn't get out! And their kids won't ever see them again."

Your child is struggling to understand the pain of other people and that struggle hurts him as well. He has empathy and he demonstrates just how complicated this ability can be. You want him to have it and so you join with him in feeling badly for the people who perished and their children. Then you help him move ahead with the knowledge that you understand his deepest feelings and these feelings are a good part of being a human being.

Step Eight: "No!!!" and Self Control

"Up, up!" Mike sits in the cart as Marla pushes it around the grocery store. At 23 months he looks older, more like a mini 5 year old in his jeans and tee shirt. From his perspective the shelves are full of things that he is familiar with; cereal boxes, rice, cookies in animal shapes. He's looking, listening to Mom's voice saying "We need this" and "we have this at home."

Mike is getting a bit weary, and bored. And then it happens. THE TOY appears! In his mind there is a flash of memory. He knows this TOY! He saw it on TV and a kid was playing with THE TOY. For Mike, it doesn't matter when this commercial was shown. It doesn't matter that THE TOY is for older kids and needs an engineer to put it together. HERE IT IS!!

Now Mike knows exactly what to do. Point, share and say what he wants, right?

"Mommy, look THE TOY!"

Marla recognizes the toy on the shelf in all its glory.

"Yes it is that toy you saw on TV." She says calmly.

"Get the toy?" Mike looks into her eyes with that incredible yearning expression"

"Not today, Mike. Let's finish shopping…."

Suddenly something feels bad inside. Mike doesn't really comprehend what this all means. All that he understands is the "not" part. Around him life goes on and Mom starts to wheel the cart down the aisle. For Mike, the sudden shift in mood inside him is unbearable and he bursts into sobs.

"Shhush, Sweetie" Marla says stroking his head.

"No!!!" Mike says brushing her hand aside. He flops to the side and Marla has to take him out of the cart before he throws himself out. She carries him screaming out of the store. Now the situation is worse because Mike is moving even farther away from THE TOY. He's so worked up at this point that he can't calm down for awhile. He won't let Marla soothe him either. "No" he says each time she tries to pat him and he struggles when she straps him into the car seat.

Mara drives home with a sobbing, red faced youngster who looks like he's about to pass out from his emotional explosion. She fights her urge to turn around and get THE TOY. She keeps glancing over at him watching his chest heave, and worries about him having a cardiac arrest. By the time they get home he's stopped sobbing but he's not a happy camper. He still is resistive to anything she says or does. Later on he refuses dinner except to drink milk. And then another fit of crying before he goes to bed. He allows Dan to read him a story and finally sleeps.

What an emotional ordeal for the parent, the child and the store manager! And yet, in this stage of the development game, between the tantrums and the trials, the child is learning about self-control. For parents the reality is that sometimes you can see the growth and often you can't. That is unless you know where to look for your child's blossoming self-control strategies.

Mike's ability to **express** negative emotion is not a new thing. He has, in fact done it in many ways from infancy and we have not wanted to suppress his capacity to **express** anger, fear, and sadness. It was a "good thing" we said, for the baby to have this ability to communicate emotions so that others could respond to him and so that the feelings didn't get all bottled up inside. At 9 months Mike had a screaming fit when Marla left him for an hour with Dan. For some reason, he didn't want her to leave on that particular day and even though he loves his father, it just wasn't enough. He cried the whole time that she was away. Dan was worn out when she came home. But he was just a baby; small and soft and well…physically manageable. Now he's bigger, stronger and louder. A parent can't just scoop him up and plop him into a crib. That's one problem for parents and the other is their expectations of what he should be able to do. His memory and cognition are more developed at 23 months right? He has *empathy* for goodness sake. Why can't he feel his mother's pain and stop the tantrum! Why can't he know how to deal with his negative feelings? All he seems to understand is "NO!"

Here is where the going gets tough. Mike can **express** negative emotions, but he doesn't know as yet **how to deal with them in other ways**. There is a difference between expressing and managing strong, overwhelming, negative and positive feelings. This is what he needs to learn at this stage of the game. When this lesson has been learned then Mike will have the capacity for self control under his belt.

For many parents it seems that all the wonderful progress towards self control has flown out of the window at this stage. It's all gone now and the terrible twos have reduced the child and parents to emotional chaos. It is hard to believe that out of this chaos will emerge superior emotional skills. One reason is that it's just so embarrassing and exhausting when your child throws a fit in public.

Barb is bringing little Brandon with her to the hospital today. It is bring your youngster to work day at the General Hospital where she is a medical professional. Brandon is all dressed up in the cutest outfit that she could buy. He didn't want to get up or get dressed this morning and the whole thing was a battle. But here they are with other doctors, nurses and their kids of all ages.

Little Brandon is a tall, sturdy child and

pretty strong for his age. Barb can't wait to show him off. She hopes that by some magic or good will on his part the youngster will "behave".

Brandon has other things in mind. If only she could know what was going on inside that brain as he looks around for an escape route. Brandon still enjoys making his own pathways when he wants to do so. Now, with his mother chatting to other people he definitely wants to explore. He makes a beeline for a table and scoots underneath. When Barb tries to pull him out he grabs the tablecloth and the whole thing crashes down.

As people watch, Brandon resists getting out of the mess and then has a tantrum when Barb pulls him up by the arms. He kicks out and a doctor yells "Ouch!"

It's hard to tell at this point who is actually having the tantrum. Barb is so embarrassed that she is red-faced and yelling at Brandon who is purple faced and screaming. Her co-workers try to intervene but Brandon is not giving in and is on the floor thrashing around.

"It's OK" Barb hears someone say. "He'll get over it just don't pay attention."

"Oh no that's not the way to do it." She overhears her boss say. "You have to do that time out thing. Don't let this kind of behavior go on even for a minute!"

After several more infuriating minutes Barb manages to half drag, half carry Brandon out of the room and put him into the car. And there he sits just like nothing has happened. Barb is in tears as she drives home. She's angry at Brandon for failing her, at her colleagues for finding out that she is a bad mother and at herself for being a bad mother.

And so where are the milestones at this stage of the game? For many youngsters we see the progress in the child's testing and learning how and when and where he or she can **express negative emotions**. They are in the youngster's learning new strategies for coping with these strong, intense feelings without exploding or imploding. As in the anecdote above parents have to have enormous abilities to overcome embarrassment when their child acts out and then teach positive ways of expressing negative emotion. Parents have to look at the periods of time between the storms as well as dealing with the storms themselves.

Parents are challenged at this time to use their own self-control skills as models for teaching the best way to harness the energy of the roller coaster of emotions.

Young children get overwhelmed with feelings, wants, and needs. As infants in all the preceding steps, parents became quite adept at soothing and finding the baby's comfort zone before the roller coaster went out of control.

Do you remember that you encouraged the baby to explore, to share and to enjoy things out loud?

Now that the child is bigger, mobile, remembering things he sees, wanting things that are far away or just out of reach, the parent cannot always comfort and soothe. It simply doesn't work for a 23 month old who doesn't have any understanding of what *"later" or "next week" or "too expensive"* means. And so this child will express his negative emotions in ways that look and sound and feel bigger, louder and more visible to the world.

At this vital stage the child's greatest achievement will be learning to express negative emotion in ways that are more acceptable to those around him. And it isn't easy. Parents tend to expect a lot from kids of this age because they talk and walk and feed themselves. The youngster will, through this phase, test out many ways of managing negative emotions and it will test your patience. In order for him to gain self control he must learn by trial and error what to do with his negative emotions when they are overwhelming.

And here are the milestones of this age. What parents can look for in this stage are the youngster's efforts to use other **positive**

strategies than "No!" or temper tantrums to deal with frustration. These positive efforts or strategies usually fall into 4 categories. They are the basic strategies that we use to harness the roller coaster of emotions and respond appropriately to the situation.

We call them *D.S.R.O.*

1. The ability to delay a response after a strong negative or positive emotional trigger. Key word here is after

2. The ability to self-soothe

3. The ability to refocus the emotional energy; by considering the big picture, or looking at some part of the situation.

4. The ability to organize thinking and problem-solve.

Look hard for these strategies as they pop up during this phase. We will be showing you what these strategies look like as we go along because each child may demonstrate them differently.

Even adults have a hard time with this aspect of self control. Expressing anger, fear and sadness has never been an easy task and many people come into therapy for advice and guidance on this issue. For children to begin to learn this skill it is imperative that the steps leading up to this are in place. The child must have a caring trusting adult around, he or she should be able to share emotions and to know how to read and understand other individual's emotional expressions. Finally the child should want to comfort others and **belong to the social and emotional world around him**.

The smartest of parents can over-react or under react to children whose trial and error attempts seen to interfere with daily life. In this regard a great deal has been written about spanking and other kinds of physical discipline. During the 'terrible Twos" the child's behavior can seriously unbalance parents and those who have self control problems of their own may be at risk for over reacting. Negative physical outbursts on the part of parents may stun a child into temporary compliance but the long term use of corporal punishment is grim indeed. Stunning, scaring and causing pain to a child does not teach him strategies for controlling his own negative emotions. This is not new information but the prevalence of abuse of children at this age remains a significant problem. Given the pressures that parents face, there must be a constant awareness that loosing one's grip on self control is always possible.

Under-reacting to the child's outbursts does not instruct him or her on how to manage negative emotions. However, it is important to *time* your responses so that the child is able to hear and learn from what you teach.

In Marla's case, she remained calm and was able to wait a while before she dealt with the problem. In her understanding of Mike's temperament, Marla knows that when he's in the heat of an outburst he isn't going to grasp her lessons at all. We will follow up on what she does in the section on exercises.

It may well be that the least effective technique for teaching your child how to deal with negative emotions is demonstrated below.

The day after Brandon's tantrum at work Barb is on the phone with his father who is a surgeon. The couple is separated but they communicate daily by phone and these contacts are very important to Barb. At this moment she is talking about her crazy work schedule and Brandon is in the next room.

> *"I'm just going to tell my boss that I....Brandon stop that!"*
>
> *Brandon has come in and is pulling on the phone cord. His face is flushed and excited.*
>
> *"I want it." He says pointing to something on the counter.*
>
> *"Let me talk to Daddy for a minute." Barb says pleadingly*
>
> *Brandon tugs at the cord again. Then he tries to drag a chair over to the counter to get the box of cookies he has seen. He's starting to whine and when he can't seem to position the chair he starts crying.*

"Hold on, Steve." Barb puts the phone down opens the cookie packet and gives one to Brandon.

"Sorry" she says to Brandon's father "He had to have that cookie"

Brandon comes over and wipes crumbs on Barbs skirt. Then he tugs at the phone in her hand.

"No, Brandon! That's enough. Go and play. Let me talk for a minute."

Brandon still has his hand on the phone as Barb stands up taking it out of his reach He begins to wail. She gives him the phone and he slams it against the table. Then she takes the phone away and tells Steve that she will call when Brandon is asleep.

Barb puts Brandon in his room and tells him to stay inside. This is a "time out" she explains to him and to herself as he throws his body against the door in protest.

The sound starts to unravel Barb's sense of purpose. She listens to Brandon hurl himself against the wood one more time. Then she opens the door and lets him run out.

Feedback is the word we're looking for to describe what happens above. *Inconsistent Feedback* is what Barb is giving to Brandon and it teaches him the wrong lesson about how to manage his emotions. Barb pays attention to his demands, then says "no" then ignores his behavior, then gives in when he cries and finally attempts to show him who is boss in the house. After all this she gives up entirely! Who is teaching what here? Very confusing and in fact it leads to more demands and more explosions.

So what should parents do in order to teach kids how to express negative emotion and how not to express it as the situation demands? What in the world does a toddler know about doing something else with his passions?

In reality you the parents have been teaching him these tricks all along! Now it is time to identify them as positive strategies for self-control and use them effectively.

If you need a reminder about all the wonderful techniques you taught him we can describe them to you. Notice, if you will, that they fall into those 4 important categories of self-control strategies (delay, self-soothe, refocus and organize). Here they are.

When you comforted your baby you demonstrated **self-soothing** techniques and they were stored in his memory right? When you left him with a sitter for a couple of hours even though he wasn't too happy about it you taught him something about **delay**. It worked because you came back to him, right? When he wanted something and you managed to have him wait even for a few seconds by distracting him you helped him **refocus**. And all of this tiny problem solving that *you* did was a model for how to **organize** one's thinking and work towards a goal.

It is OK that you didn't know that you were preparing him in this exact way. Parents usually don't think in terms of the 4 categories when they are in the middle of a crisis. Now that you know what you did, you can look for evidence of these strategies in your child. It may be hard to find but if your child is not having tantrums every hour he is doing some of these things. Remember to look at the child when he isn't on the roller coaster. You will see evidence of the four strategies.

Marla is a brave person. She decided to take Mike to the store again the following week! But before they took that journey she worked to teach Mike what to do when he wanted something that couldn't have. She started very slowly with this project. She started with a book that he said he wanted to look at. This particular book was an album of pictures that she and Dan took down once in awhile. It was not an everyday book and not something that she would simply hand over to him and walk away.

Mike made it very clear that he really, really wanted to see THE BOOK. Marla told him gently that this activity would have to wait until his father got home. Mike was OK for about a minute. Then he started to demand THE BOOK.

Marla told him about the plan to wait for his father to come home. "NO!" Mike said and was ready to cry. Marla simply left the room and began to fold clothes in the bedroom. She put on the TV and watched as she folded. It was very quiet in the living room. Mike had lost his audience and no one was going to argue with him. He was still angry, of course but interested in what Mom was doing. He came into the bedroom and sullenly plopped down on the bed to watch TV. It was 3:00 only two hours until Dan was do to come home. Two long hours, Marla thought. Perhaps too long.

After an hour of watching TV Marla got a phone call from Dan. He was going to be late. She made a decision at that point and told Mike that his father was delayed. Mike's eyes filled with tears. But he waited. "You've been good about waiting." Marla said. "I think we can take a look at that book before he comes home."

Mike's expression was priceless. He radiated pure joy, relief, surprise and a sense of accomplishment.

A small victory, you might say but every time a child of this age can **delay** getting what he wants, can be **distracted and refocus on some other activity** for awhile and use **self soothing techniques** such as staying close to the person he loves, it's an important step towards self- control. These are the strategies that work now and later on in managing the roller coaster of emotions in life.

Children of this age will, in many different ways, seek out your help in resolving the emotional dilemma. For the parent it is a matter of knowing your child and watching and listening to what he is saying .He may simply join you in an activity (watching TV) or sit by you or talk to you. Seeking your help and being soothed by you are not failures in self- control. They are successful ways that adults use to control fluctuating emotions.

A child's statement of "no" and his resistance to doing something he doesn't *want* to do, may or may not be followed by a tantrum. When the youngster is *not* a thrower of fits parents may do well to ignore some of the behavior. Parents who loose control themselves when a child is negative are giving the wrong message and not teaching self control skills. Ignoring may take some of the wind out of the child's resistance. If you can walk away and not explode, maybe he will learn not to "sweat the small stuff"

Self control is not a matter of shutting down the child's emotions and teaching him how to shut down his own feelings.

Constant and intense tantrums are a red flag for parents. It signals a real breakdown in self control development and should be taken seriously. Children of this age who explode frequently often have other symptoms that indicate they are on a perpetual roller coaster of emotion. These problems may pop up as sleep disorders, feeding disorders, toilet training disorders and language delays.

When you have medically ruled out any physical problems with your child that may contribute to the above disturbances it may be helpful to consider missed steps in the youngsters self control learning process.

Here is a case from the author's work with a child who is suspected of having ADHD.

Jennie brought 23 month old Adam into the clinic because his 3rd babysitter quit. The sitter said that Adam's constant tantrums left her exhausted and she simply didn't know what to do with him. Jennie has to work. She is a single Mom with no available family to help with Adam.

When they are in the quiet office, Adam focuses only on the toy box and pulls toys out with alarming speed. His mother sits with her hands tightly clasped in her lap.

"I'm sorry for the mess he's making." She says softly. She looks over at him and then back at the interviewer.

The interviewer sits and watches. Jennie is very anxious. Adam is very busy. Then he runs to her and pulls on her hand. "Out, out go home!" he says loudly.

"No, Adam we have to stay here and answer the questions first."

Jennie looks at Adam with a tense expression on her face. She is very ashamed and anxious. Adam pushes her away and goes back to the toys. After a minute or two Adam rushes to her and pulls on her hand. Jennie looks at the interviewer for help. She doesn't know what to do at this point. Adam is getting the upper hand by expressing negative emotion aggressively. Jennie is miserable and embarrassed. Their faces, voices and body language shout out the reality that they are both on the roller coaster without any control.

In this case what helped both mother and child was to work on Jennie's ability to see his positive behaviors amidst the chaos and to build attachment and sharing abilities. In reading this case did anyone catch the part where Adam **listened** to his mother and went back to the toys? It was only briefly but he was able to use some healthy self-control strategies right there. Did Jennie see this? When she takes him into a new and strange office environment she might be able to anticipate some exploratory behaviors on his part and help him in a protective way to look around together. They can share what they see and find before getting down to business. A parent is in charge of her child whether they are in a doctor's office, a store or a friend's home. With a high energy child like Adam it is important to help them explore, to show them that you are the one that they are bonded to and should look to for directions.

This little case illustrates the importance of looking back as well as ahead on the journey to self-control. Adam is attached to his mother and she gradually learned to use this bond and his ability to share emotional expressions when she taught him strategies for self-control.

Jennie also learned to value herself as a mother, and to practice and model healthy self-control strategies.

Now Jennie looks for positive behaviors and expects that Adam will go forward instead of backwards.

In earlier sections we talked about the fact that the parent's expectations and perceptions of the child's behavior have quite an impact upon what that child will actually do. In this difficult stage parents who are having a difficult time with teaching self control strategies often see their toddlers as somehow unresponsive to them. It certainly appears as though the child couldn't care less about your feelings, your needs and shows this to the entire world in his tantrums and negativity. This view may go even deeper and influence the child's development.

Barb has gotten pretty frustrated with Brandon and the advice she gets isn't helping. Even his father, Steven seems to believe that it's all her fault. And Brandon, he obviously doesn't love her anymore. He made that clear over and over again. Barb feels totally rejected by her own child and this is terribly painful for her. Being rejected is something she's always fought against. She needs to be appreciated. Now it seems that when she thinks about Brandon or considers taking him somewhere she hasn't the strength to endure another explosive expression of "I hate you Mom." She distances herself from him more and more as she expects that her relationship with him has become somehow toxic.

Now, of course, Barb can't teach him anything. And there is a lot of data in the scientific realm to show that children of parents who feel rejected in this way tend to become more aggressive as they grow older. They become less and less able to cope with negative emotions in appropriate ways. This does grave damage to their self esteem and their ability to get along with others.

It is at this age that parents find their children becoming more peer oriented. Teaching the strategies for self control will enable the child to engage with other kids in a healthy manner. Parents don't want their children to hit, bite, yell and fight. Having an aggressive youngster is a constant dilemma even before he enters school On the other hand parents don't want their kids to be victims of these aggressive kids. Youngsters who cannot cope with negative emotions and strong levels of excitement can become targets for other kids to pick on. Becoming a victim this early does not bode well for the future.

The Terrible Two's are a time of turbulence and a time for growth. This is the nature of most "crisis" situations and child development is no different. Parents can use their continued "power" as adults to teach and shape behavior before the youngster is expected to function at the higher level of school and in competitive peer group activities.

This is an excellent time to look at your child's temperament and see where he or she is on the excitability scale. Many children are high energy at this stage of the game but are learning about self-control. Being active and curious is normal at this stage. Youngsters who are still very easily excited and irritable may require more help learning the strategies.

A New Temperament Evaluation

Below are descriptions of behavior. How often does your child do the following?

	Always	Sometimes	Never
1.acts restless, (squirmy)			
2.. makes noises when he shouldn't			
3. is demanding			
4. doesn't stay on task (finish)			
5. or fights with other kids			
6. pouts and sulks			
7. has trouble sleeping			
8. has temper tantrums			
9. acts bossy with others			
10 blames others; denies responsibility			

	Always	Sometimes	Never
11. daydreams or acts 'out of it'			
12. has eating problems (very picky)			
13. Looks wound up; tight facial expression or body language			

Items 4, 5, 8,9,10 and 13 are very important. If you rated **always** on these particular items please focus on the exercises below.

Self control Exercises

Use play and imagination to teach the four techniques: delay, self soothe, refocus and organize. At this age, children who can use language to express themselves should be encouraged to do so during these exercises.

1. Figure or doll enactment; try using dolls or action figures to play out the scenes where the child-figure has to use the strategies in order to get something. It can also be the adult figure who has to delay. Example; the Puppy Game. In this game the child figure (or doll) wants to bring home a lost puppy and Mom doesn't know about it. The child has to figure out how to tell Mom about the puppy, how to keep puppy quiet in the garage, how to delay bringing puppy into the house until Mom accepts the idea etc. etc.
2. Read stories about kids who have to wait for something and what they do to remain calm. Make one up.
3. Counting games; Let Mom count to 3 before child says the magic word (pretzel). And get a reward (the pretzel). Then let Mom count to 6 and then 10 and so on.
4. The stop and go game. Red light green light and winner follows the directions. Can be done with one parent who says red or green and the child has to stop and then take a step with each direction.
5. The competitive game; parent and child simple board game in which playing is the goal and not winning. Reward the child for sticking with the game when things get tough.
6. Model self control strategies for your child (the four categories) and verbalize what you are doing.
7. Use language; teach the child other ways of expressing the negative emotions. Instead of "No"! How about "Not now, please" or a simple "I'm tired now" or Can I do it a little later, please?"
8. Return to the earlier steps and do a bit of face to face interaction, have a special time to share with the child, and to explore with the youngster.

This is a difficult stage for many parents and children. It is important to avoid shaming or harshly blaming the child for the many things that he or she may do to rock the boat. It is also not healthy for parents to be ashamed and blame themselves. Use each crisis as a starting point for learning self-control skills. You and your youngster will benefit from this experience.

You move up from this Step with *powerful* techniques that you can use to help your youngster manage his emotions. D.S.R.O. is a newly developed system that guides you towards the positive behaviors your child is demonstrating in the domain of self- control. Your child will face many experiences that push his negative emotion buttons. Even though he has empathy and a growing understanding of his own feelings and the feelings of others your youngster needs guidance in how to express and deal with anger, frustration and fear. Negative emotions are a normal part of our human adaptive gear and the energy that these feelings contain has to be harnessed in positive ways. As we will see in the next step the ability to manage or control this energy will serve his growing memory abilities. We recommend that parents take time to consider the following points:

1. Your child is learning how to express feelings by watching not only you but other people on TV, movies etc. It is important to review what he is looking at and learning from in terms of expressing anger, fear and frustration. There is a great deal of TV content that shows people impulsively acting on anger by fighting and yelling. This is not conducive to your child's learning adaptive ways of expressing his emotions.
2. Actively watch how your youngster expresses negative as well as positive feelings after viewing TV or movies and consider limiting his exposure.
3. Use the D.S.R.O system and help your child with the strategies of self control.

A Sneak Preview; Imagine your child 15 years from now. He is a teenager and he is faced with enormous social pressures as well as academic and emotional challenges. You worked hard to teach him how to handle his anger when he was a small child and it was tough. He had a temper then and he does have one now. And now he is bigger and stronger than you are. You will depend upon those early lessons to help him through this difficult time without exploding in destructive ways. The day comes when you have to tell him that he is not going out with his friends because he got a failing grade in math. This is a crisis for him and for you. He is enraged. He stomps around the kitchen. He calls his friend and complains. He tells you that you are not "being fair." And suddenly, just for a moment his anger abates and he looks worried. During that important pause you see the 2 year old child again and wonder what he is going to do. Then he takes a deep breath and says, "Well I can't understand the math so I need a tutor or something."

This is one thing that you taught him. You wanted him to deal with his anger by reaching out for help when he needed it. Now that he is on the roller coaster he is seeking that help and with your support he can find his emotional balance. This is a milestone in the development of emotional intelligence. If this adolescent can maintain his cool and use the tools you have given him in other situations then he is closer than ever to achieving the ultimate goal of emotional intelligence.

Step Nine: Memory and Self-Control

"Who is this child?" Dan said only half kidding as he watched Mike play ball in the front yard. They stood at the window ready to go outside if needed. Mike was directing three other kids as though he was the manager of a baseball team. Cathy, Ed and a new boy on the block all appeared to be listening to him and following his directions. They used plastic bats and balls that Dan had purchased several weeks before. Then chaos erupted as the new kid threw his bat at Cathy. She looked like she might cry and then she jumped on the new boy. At that moment Dan was running out the door and he heard Mike yell "Stop or I call the police!"

It was an interesting statement from an almost 3 year old. Dan managed to settle things down and stayed outside. He found that he had to monitor the new kid who really wanted to play but had no clue how to take turns.

A week later Marla overheard Mike telling the story to his grandmother on the phone.

"And gramma." He said in a serious tone "I showed my friends how to play and this boy did a bad thing and I got worried and he didn't stop it and Dad came."

Marla waited and Mike said "Yes, I did a right thing. Dad said so. I was good. That boy is bad. He lives next door!"

Another long pause and Mike laughed. "I forgot. He's not all bad. I have to show him how to play, right?"

"Who is this child?" Marla thought to herself as she listened in. Sometimes I can almost see how he is going to be later on in life. I can really see a little personality there. He's his own man, so to speak.

There is no definitive day on which a child's strengths and weaknesses come together in some kind of a package that endures over time. This personality package is known as *the self* and it is an entity that the child recognizes over time. The child's *self* is not physically part of the parent or the friends or anyone else. The emotions and behaviors of this "self" is what the child will be controlling for the rest of his or her life.

We have one big clue as to when *this self* may really be solidifying into a whole that has a past, a present and a future. When we take a closer look at Mike's use of language we can see that he uses words to announce his future intentions; what he plans to do (call the police, or help the new kid). Future time now exists and he can see himself in this future and doing things! Mike also has a view of himself in past experiences and he refers to this with his grandmother when he retells the story of the game and what happened. These are emotionally loaded experiences for him and they have become part of his memory. He will draw upon these experiences as he continues to learn to control his feelings and his behavior.

The development of memory, the emergence of the self and self-control is intimately related. Children and adults rely on their past successes or failures in important situations. These memories are templates for present and future strategies for managing emotions.

At around Mike's age children show that they are developing what is called *autobiographical memory*. This is the incredible capacity that enables them to recognize themselves as individuals in past events. With this ability they can link events and themselves in time sequence, and begin to see cause and consequence in brighter light. The dramatic growth in memory capacity provides the child with more data that he can use in the management of his emotions and behavior.

Children of Mike's age talk in a way that shows the emergence of autobiographical memory as we see in the anecdote above. Listen to them carefully and you might hear the important words; **"I remember" or I forgot"**

The reality is that memories for children at this age are very emotionally driven. They become embedded and influence the development of the child. Kids recall experiences in which they have had pain or pleasure more directly than other memories. Remembering painful past events at this time may well influence the techniques that they use to control their feelings and behavior. The key positive strategies that they are still learning to apply; *delay, distraction, self soothing* and *organizing thinking* can be undermined when the child recalls having painful emotional experiences with a parent or other caring adult when his self control abilities failed. At that point if the child remembers being abused, shamed, harshly punished, rejected the scenarios remain locked into memory.

Let us take a look at a case from our practice that gets dramatically to the point.

Cara is a victim of child abuse (emotional and physical) from a very young age. Her memory doesn't go back before age 3 or 4 but the uncle who perpetrated the abuse was in the home when she was 2 years old. The abuse was in the form of harsh punishment by hitting and name calling when Cara didn't do what she was supposed to do. The uncle was her babysitter while the family was running a small grocery store. Cara's parents spent a great deal of time in their business and the uncle was one of her primary caretakers. He wasn't abusive all of the time, just when he was feeling bad and couldn't sneak a drink.

Cara's parents described her as a quiet child, with a tendency towards thumb sucking and difficulty getting her up and dressed in the morning. In fact she had to be forced into her clothes by Mom before she left for the store. In kindergarten, Cara was labeled a "day dreamer" but there seemed to be no cause for alarm. Her pediatrician noticed that she had a tendency to bite her nails and pick at scabs but she was generally in good health. Her parents were doing well financially and they could finally afford a sitter after school and the uncle left when she was 6 years old. Cara's problems in school were not the kind to ring any bells. She remained a "day dreamer", did average work when she remembered her homework and mostly liked to be by herself.

We saw Cara when she was 10 years of age, in the emergency room. Her mother brought her in because Cara was making deep grooves in the skin of her arms. She was also obese for her age and sneaking food into her room.

Mother was now able to be at home more and she had come upon Cara cutting herself with a scissor on her bed. The marks had been hidden under long sleeves but some looked to be months old, even years old and others were fresh. Her mother found out about the uncle's hitting and name calling only indirectly. It turned out that he abused another child after he left Cara's home and he was then shunned by the family.

Cara was a pretty girl, definitely chunky but dressed nicely. She was calm and cooperative and very difficult to evaluate. The primary reason for this was that Cara couldn't or didn't want to talk about the early abuse. She said that "she didn't remember" or that it was "not interesting". When asked why she cut herself she said "It makes me feel better. I don't know why. I can stop anytime."

She responded to questions about sneaking food by saying "my mother's making a big deal about nothing." Cara had a superficial calm about her that was hard to penetrate. She maintained a bored look on her face, or smiled, or looked at the TV.

The important concern for this young girl at that time was; would she continue to cut her arms and eventually do permanent damage? Unless we could get inside her mind and explore her feelings we knew that changing this behavior was an impossible goal.

"Why does she cut herself?" her mother asked.

"Cara cuts herself because she has intense, uncomfortable feelings inside her that she cannot cope with. It's like she's on a roller coaster of emotions that she can't control. There's probably fear and shame and anger inside of her." This is part of the answer.

"But cutting? How does that help her cope with the feelings?" is her mother's next question.

This is the hard one because we have to assume from the history that Cara picked up this technique in some form quite early and in response to painful emotional experiences. She found that it gave her some control over the pain that she was experiencing. Cutting relieves the inner stress in some way and she is in charge of when and how she does it.

Simply put, this is not a healthy strategy for self control but it works for her. She isn't exploding in rage is she? She's not really bothering anyone, right? And she gets into some kind of a Comfort Zone. This is not the only strange strategy that children learn and keep doing when they have little or no opportunity to learn the other methods. Somehow they have to cope with unpleasant or even very intensely pleasant emotional experiences and keep on going.

Cara's case may seem to be an extreme one in light of your own family experiences. And yet when young children are in the process of building that self-image that will endure over time there are *little* things that can have a big impact and be stored into memory.

Small traumas can upset the child's ability to get back into a comfort zone and remain locked in memory. The child who struggles with sudden, unpredictable, negative emotional events and cannot find a way to cope may turn to unhealthy strategies and then repeat them...and repeat them.

Do you remember Bob? Of course you do. Well he seemed to be progressing well enough since his mother became pregnant and her anxiety became focused on other issues. Then tragedy struck and her husband was hospitalized for a serious medical problem that was suspected to be chronic. Bob was 3 years old at this time.

Bob loved his father. This was the person who knew where his *comfort zone* was. Dad let him be himself and just his presence in the evening somehow reduced the anxiety in the household. He loved to play with his father in the evening. It made things fun and Bob called upon these memory-feelings whenever he was stressed or unhappy. He had a *good memory* for his happy times with Dad and he used it.

Now Dad was gone and there was a terrible anxious pressure in the house. Bob did, at first, spend a lot of time remembering the good things. He drew pictures of his Dad and he made up stories but Mom just wasn't interested. The pressure grew inside and one day in pre-school he hit a kid who wouldn't give him a ball. The child didn't fight back but ran off and told the teacher. Bob had done this only twice before when he was feeling bad and both times his mother yelled at him when he got home. His father had talked to him about it and then let it go. Bob was able to maintain some self-control and keep going.

Bob's nervousness increased as he got off the school bus on the day he hit the kid. He entered the house. He was scared about being yelled at. This time Mom didn't seem to get upset and he felt a wave of relief. There it was. It was a feeling that was better than anxiety, better than what he had been experiencing over the past few weeks. It became something of a game and a challenge and a distraction for Bob to do small bad things and then get away with them. The feeling of relief after the build up of tension always made him feel good. When his father came home, still ill and bed-ridden, Bob continued with this method of coping with his fears and anxieties because *it worked for him*. It became part of his behavior repertoire and a way of finding comfort in a very uncomfortable situation. It helped him to manage the roller coaster of feelings in a very unhealthy way. But it worked for him until later on when he did get caught.

The feelings of anxiety, fear, sadness and anger can become overwhelming even for kids who have already developed strategies for managing these emotions. Children in the 3 year age range who are developing a self identity are still at risk for learning and remembering unhealthy techniques for managing emotional pain. And the reality is that these habits become deeply ingrained because of their maturing memory and cognitive abilities.

Parents have to try and be aware and to evaluate **situations** around their children for things that may upset their capacity to manage the roller coaster of feelings. The tragedy of Sept. 11 was one that spread from adults to children who were too young to fully understand what was going on. Many parents believe that 3 year olds don't understand the meaning of death and they may be correct. However, youngsters do understand and react to their parents and other adult's expressions of fear and rage when a massive crisis occurs. They get scared and angry too and their ability to cope with these strong feelings that are all around and inside of them is limited. And they remember the situations in which these feelings were intense and overwhelming. After Sept. 11 there many children who couldn't manage the stress and reverted to old babyish habits such as bed wetting, night terrors, tantrums. Some unfortunately are still unable to cope and we are sure that we will see them in the near future with problematic ways of managing fear and anger.

When a child's memory pops up with something that upsets his self-control strategies it is useful for parents to use their own memory abilities to recall past events. The child may be remembering himself in a past situation that was anxious, fearful or frightening for some reason. The child can't usually put this all together and tell you about the fact that he is on the roller coaster again. Something small or something very dramatic may have occurred months ago that your child is having problems with and is showing you by loosing control in key areas. In this way bed-wetting, tantrums, sleeping problems may pop up seemingly out of the blue. Parents can take a look at past events to see what may have triggered the child's response and then help them get back into a comfort zone.

The following is a questionnaire that may help parents get a sense of how the child's **memory** abilities and **self** concept are progressing.

Questionnaire

1   When offered a little prize now or a bigger one later my child will
     probably
      (a)   opt for big one later on
      (b)   take the one now
      (c)   unsure

2. My child uses the words remember or forget
      (a)   often
      (b)   not at all
      (c)   unsure

3. When my child plays she seems to reenact things that happened before.
- (a)   often
- (b)   never
- (c)   don't know

4. When we talk to my child about his behavior after it occurs he
- (a)   seems to learn from it
- (b)   makes fun
- (c)   ignores it

5. My child likes when I tell stories about when he was "a baby" and the cute things he did
- (a)   often
- (b)   rarely
- (c)   never

6. When there is a delay in getting something he wants my child
- (a)   usually asks why and tries to wait
- (b)   asks why and gets angry
- (c)   immediately gets out of hand

7. My child seems to have some purpose or goal in mind when he does something
- (a)   often
- (b)   rarely
- (c)   never

8. My child seems to be in his own little world.
- (a)   never
- (b)   rarely
- (c)   always

9. My child likes to try different ways to saying things.
- (a)   always
- (b)   sometimes
- (c)   never

Children at this age will demonstrate in play and in language that their memory skills are working along with their self control capacities. For this mini questionnaire, parents who had 7 or more (b) and (c) answers should try the exercises below with the understanding that your child's memory development is not at the same level as everyone else's memory.

Exercises to improve self control strategies using the child's developing memory and language capacities

1. Easy Raisin Game. Tell the child that he can have 1 raisin (or a candy or penny) right now or 5 of them if he waits a minute. If the child chooses to wait then give the reward and explain that he has just won a self control game. You can do this with other objects (pennies) and gradually increase the delay time!

2. Advanced Raisin Game. Tell the child that he can have one penny right now or 5 pennies when he picks up his toys. This rewards delay of gratification and cooperation with parent. You can use this to help him to do other chores and gradually increase the amount of work he has to do to get the reward. You may also substitute non money non food rewards such as a gold star, or TV time etc.

3. The rehearsal exercise. Help the child construct a fantasy about a situation where there is a choice between a long term big goal and a short term little reward. Let the child imagine out loud about how he might delay gratification to get to the big prize.

4. Do a task together build a model; let the child guide you and reward his persistence, his ability to be flexible and in control.

5. Reflecting exercise. Read a story, stopping and allowing the child to tell you what he understands. Do this repeatedly so that the stopping and reflecting become a pattern.

Having *a self* to control is truly a monumental thing. It is easier when your little self is part of your parents and they have all the responsibility for stabilizing emotions and behavior.

Remembering yourself in situations when you have lost control is another big issue. How much we as adults, would love to forget the time we lost it and exploded in the face of someone we care about. If only we could block out that image of what we did in front of our co-workers! It would be so good not to worry in advance about loosing it in the future!

Memory and having a self concept makes things harder and yet we can use these experiences to teach children how to use positive strategies and to learn from each situation.

You move up from this Step prepared with the *latest research-driven* information on memory and how it relates to self control. Sometimes we appreciate the capacity of memory only after we are exposed to someone who has lost this capacity entirely. We know now that individuals with deteriorated memories are "not themselves" any longer. These people flounder in a world that is emotionally confusing and they often cannot control their behavior. They have no remembered **self** to control, no memory for the strategies that they once used and no way to learn and remember complicated new techniques.

As painful as this is we also know that memory has to be stimulated and nurtured from infancy through old age. We cannot take for granted that this wonderful capacity will remain intact. And we have learned that it can be harmed by such things as constant stress and exposure to violence. In this regard we ask parents to do the following.

1. Monitor your child's exposure to violence on TV, movies and videos etc. Research has demonstrated that memory is impacted by exposure to violence on the screen. Please refer to our safe internet sites in the Resource Section.

2. Do use safe and time-tested memory boosters such as photo albums, family videos and story telling about the child's grand-parents and other significant people.

A Sneak Preview; Imagine your youngster 5 years from now. She is sitting in the living room with the family album spread out on her lap. Her small fingers turn the pages. She smiles softly and bends over a picture. She presses her little lips to the photo. Last week her grand father passed away and your child is struggling with this loss. She loved her grand father and this is the first member of the family to pass away.

"Mom?" She says. She sees you standing there watching her. "Mom do you remember when Toby stopped moving and we put him in a box in the yard. Then we held hands and said a little good by poem for him?"

You do remember the death of her hamster, Toby when she was 2 years old. She had a temper tantrum after his death and it took hours to calm her down. What helped her at that time was the simple routine of the burial, the prayer and a photo album with every picture of Toby and other hamsters in it. She slept with that photo album every night for a month and still loves to bring it out.

Amazing how kids remember simple things that soothed and comforted them when they were emotionally distressed! Now you know how to use her memory to help her through this crisis without the melt down of a temper tantrum.

Step Ten: Self-Appraisal and Self-Control

Dan and Marla have invited Geraldo, Ed and Anna over for a BBQ. Mike and Ed are both three years and a few months old. Jill is 6 and she has a buddy over to play with. Dan and Geraldo first do the manly thing and go out in the yard for a few minutes and a cold beer. Marla and Anna are in the kitchen while Ed and Mike are working on a model that has to be glued together.

Dan starts the conversation with a mild "So how's it going?

Geraldo takes a long, thoughtful pull on his beer and says, "We're going to separate for awhile and see how it goes." He makes this statement without encouraging any input.

Dan watches the birds circle around for awhile and then asks, "How's the boy taking the news?"

"Don't think he knows yet." Geraldo replies. "Unless the arguing has tipped him off." He throws the can over the fence turns and walks back towards the house.

Inside the living room Mike and Ed are struggling with the model instructions which are way beyond their reading capacity.

"Forget it!" Ed says and crumbles the paper up.

"Wait. Don't do that." Mike says and tries to spread out the instructions.

"You're stupid." Ed says. "Anyway I brought that model over so it is mine and I can break it if I want."

At this moment Anna pokes her head in and asks "How's it going with the model?"

Ed starts to jump on one small piece of the plastic yelling, "Stupid, stupid, plane."

Anna rushes over and scoops him up sitting him down on the couch. Ed's starting to wail and she sits next to him, putting her arm around him and saying. "Now, now don't worry, we have other models at home and we're cooking up your favorite dinner."

Geraldo enters the living room and looks at the mess on the floor. He slowly turns his face towards Ed and Anna. There is a hard look in his eyes.

"Come over here, boy." He says to Ed. The boy doesn't leave his mother's arms.

Mike looks alarmed but steps over the mess and begins to clean it up. He has a look of grim determination on his face as he gathers the pieces of plastic.

Geraldo shakes his head and says in a loud, angry voice. "Why are you doing that for him? He has to clean up his own mess. He can't stay a baby in his Mom's arms."

Just as Dan comes in Mike's voice rings out loud and clear. "It's my house. If he can't do it, I can."

Geraldo stomps out of the room and Mike glances over at Ed with a concerned look on his voice. Ed is huddled against his mother and they both look miserable.

"Hey!" Mike says. "Let's go play ball!"

Ed wipes his eyes with his sleeve, scrambles off his mother's lap and the boys head outside. But before they are out the door, Mike asks his father one question. "Is it OK to go outside now?"

There are many wonderful facets to this scene. The point of the anecdote is not to blame Geraldo for his frustration, or to show how Anna may not be handling the situation well. Although Ed's turmoil is gut wrenching it is not the focus of our attention. Beyond all of that what we identify here is the culmination of steps in developing self control capabilities.

Incredibly, it is not only Mike who successfully uses self-control strategies during this very difficult emotional time. Ed manages to deploy a few techniques himself even though he is doing it against great odds. But he can't pull it all together like Mike does because of the many factors that are getting in Ed's and the families way.

What Mike succeeds in doing here is not only to control his own emotions and behavior but to use his intelligent mind to understand the people around him and then to solve the problem. Putting the pieces together like this, in the face of strong emotional forces means that Mike has achieved an ultimate goal in self control. That goal is to be able without direction or coercion to organize and coordinate actions towards a positive outcome. This is independent self control. This is the ability to find your own comfort zone and then solve the problem.

And oh if we could only get inside this youngster's mind! At this point in time there are so many things at work on so many levels of memory, attention, cognition, sensory processing… that we would barely be able see how Mike manages to operate the controls. He's managing so many systems with split second precision that it rivals the most advanced computer.

As we have seen, self control is so much more than the sum of its parts. It is the interaction of several strategies in a flexible manner depending upon the situation. Not all strategies are independent at all times. For example, Mike could have gone to find his mother to get help with his own anxiety about the situation. That would be a good strategy. Many kids of his age and older still seek help and that's fine. But little by little they begin to take the ball into their own hands *if* they have mastered the skills to do it. And, of course, they will succeed to a greater degree if they have the self esteem and the *self* motivation on board. Even Mike has his miserable moments as he faces different kinds of situations.

Mike awoke the morning after the barbeque feeling odd. Getting out of bed took an effort because he was still thinking about the dream he'd had. He wobbled into the bathroom and tried to pee exactly into the center of the toilet. He missed and felt his cheeks flush. "Stupid" he mumbled to himself.

During breakfast the conversation was all about Jill and the play that her class was going to do. Mike lifted a spoonful of cereal to his lips. It dribbled down his chin. "Dumb" he said to himself hoping no one caught the clumsiness. He was a big boy now and didn't like to mess up.

"Ohhh!" said Jill giggling. Look at that Mom he's making a puddle of milk. How gross!"

Mike feels bad in his stomach. He tries to mop up the milk and bumps the bowl. Cereal sloshes over. Jill is laughing merrily and Marla gets up for a sponge. Dan walks in and says, "What's all the fun about?" He sits down and Mike slumps in his chair.

"Sit up straight at the table like a big boy, Mike." Dan says casually.

Suddenly Mike's eyes begin to fill with tears of frustration. Now it's really bad and he feels like a stupid messy baby. His roller coaster emotions are taking a steep dive right at this point. Jill is talking to Dan in her best voice, sneaking peaks at his red face.

Without warning, Mike lurches from his chair so that it falls over backward. He kicks at the chair with his bare toes and it hurts. Then he says to Jill, "You are stupid and lame and dumb and ugly". He barely sees the surprised looks on his parent's faces as he dashes out of the room and throws himself on the couch.

Yes, it's a failure of the self-control system. And yes it happens frequently as children begin to use their strategies in many different emotional contexts. Expecting perfection from a child of this age is not a smart thing to do. Their world is expanding and they are called upon to deal with some pretty tough situations.

The best thing that parents can do is to give children the freedom to succeed, to test out their strengths and maybe to fail. There are things that will **boost** their self control skills as they move along.

First: it is important to keep up their self-esteem.

Second: it is vital to help them when it is necessary to get back into their Comfort Zones.

Third: parents can now teach them *how to evaluate or appraise their own behavior.*

This is the ultimate milestone capacity for this age and it is the ability to look at and appraise one's own behavior. To be self-critical in a positive way

After Mike's performance at the breakfast table his parents have the same options you would have. Especially in the rush to get ready for work and school. And so along with your priorities of getting everything ready you ask yourself.

Would it be helpful to ignore his "bad" behavior and not further harm his self esteem?

Could some constructive work be done at this point so that he can learn from this episode?

Realistically, when parents are rushed in the morning, this kind of episode has to be handled quickly so as not to set the day off on a bad track. Both questions can be answered in the affirmative as Marla demonstrates.

Marla cleans off the table, sends Jill to collect her school work, kisses Dan "good by" and stops by the couch on her way to the bedroom. Mike has his face stuffed into a pillow. It's been 10 or so minutes since he had his outburst and this down time helps in terms of ignoring the bad behavior.

"It's time to get ready for school, Mike. Need any help?"

There's a muffled "no" from the pillow

"Let's talk about this later on, Mike. We can all learn from things that we do right or wrong. Think about what you said to your sister and what you might like to tell her later on. Now it's time to move ahead with the day."

Mike slides off the couch without really looking at his mother. She gives him a quick hug and walks into her own bedroom to get dressed.

There are, indeed, many examples of how parents can handle a situation like this. They're not fancy strategies and yet they contain the important ingredients of supporting the child's self esteem, and letting the child know that there is an important lesson in this that will be useful.

What would punishment do in this situation when parents are frazzled and just need to get ready to go? Even a mild punishment (such as a threat of no TV later on) or an angry tone of voice sends a message to the child. That message is not helpful in terms of his self control skills at this age when his self esteem is so important. The message is that the parents easily react in anger and that an episode like this does not rate any evaluation by parent or child.

Teaching your child to **evaluate** his own behavior usually begins after he's done something "bad" as in loss of self control. When he's good he simply gets praise or nothing at all. It is very important, therefore to use these instances of loss of control as learning experiences. In that way the child will solve future problems involving loss of control.

Many adults, as we know, do not engage in **reflecting** over their losses in self control. It's easier to just forget about it, pretend it didn't happen, or pretend it wasn't your fault or apologize and walk away feeling bad. Self-evaluation doesn't have to be difficult or painful for child or adult when it comes to self control. Self-evaluation is more easily done when we consider the BIG PICTURE of self-control. We have to look at the four categories when we are evaluating its success or failure.

It helps to break down self control into its four parts so that the child and you can look at each one and decide how to make changes.

The D.S.R.O. Model

1. The first part is the ability to delay (inhibit or stop) the inappropriate behavior following a strong negative or positive feeling from inside or outside. These negative or positive feelings are triggers for behavior. The key word here is following and we must be aware of these triggers.

2. The second is the ability to self-soothe any inner turmoil that has been induced

3. The third is the ability to refocus the emotional energy. This may involve distancing from the problem and for a small child the easiest thing is for him to walk away for a minute and do something else.

4. The fourth is the ability to organize the thoughts so that you can solve the problem.

What is the BIG PICTURE in terms of Mike's breakdown? How can we evaluate this series of events?

When we look at Mike's behavior as his mother might, it would seem that he "lost it" at the breakfast table after Dan's remark about him being a "big boy". This looks like a failure of all factors and it is. What is more important here is to see how each part weakened so that the entire system went down.

Parents usually don't have a clue about what really sets off loss of control but they can assume that the final explosion was not the first problem. We don't have to know exactly what set the whole process of when we want to teach the child how to evaluate his performance. For Mike it is useful to remember his being taunted by Jill and Dan's statement about being a big boy and go from there. Kids at this age are trying to be "big boys and girls" and the idea of returning to the baby phase gives them bad vibes.

We now know that he couldn't stop his behavior after being triggered by the negative emotion that "baby" stimulated in him. He couldn't self soothe and refocus his attention well enough so that he could organize his thoughts into a positive mode of response. Breakdowns in the self-control system may not always involve all of the major factors but this gives us a good chance to look at the self-evaluation and the strengthening process in all of its aspects.

From what we already know, Mike has to be helped with his ability to handle being called or treated like a "baby". This taunt apparently triggers the chain of events that he can't deal with. We can approach this in general terms for any child:

1. Agree with the child that being called a baby or feeling like a messy baby is not a good feeling. This identifies the strong feeling that created the outburst. *The triggers are now clearly labeled.* Remind him that some people do hurtful things without knowing they do it.

2. Now you can move on to helping him with self soothing method.

3. Reinforce the fact that he is growing up to be big and good and helpful and he should always remember this in his mind. This is to help him with *self soothing* and add something to his memory bank for strategies.

4. Now you can move on to helping him refocus his energy on something positive.

5. Show him all of the things he does well; take him to his room where his projects are or in the kitchen where his pictures are hanging..

6. Now show him how to organize his thinking to develop a plan.

7. Help him think of ways he can deal with anyone calling him a baby or when he just feels like a baby; *this helps him organize his thinking*. Examples may be for him to say that he is not a baby, or remember that he is a big boy or to remember that he has a plan to walk away from the taunt.

8. As you move along in these steps you are showing him the parts of his self-control system that were not up to par. This is how he learns to look at the parts of his own behavior and decide that they have to be changed. This is the beginning of self-evaluation. Parents still have to guide the process.

9. Finally, explain to him that he is not to hurt other people with names or behavior and this is an important rule. This refocuses his attention on the larger social rules of any situation. In Mike's case he called his sister names and should apologize to her.

Many children learn to evaluate their own behaviors only after seeing that their parents also take responsibility for self-appraisal after a loss of control. It is useful for parents to talk about their mistakes and how they plan to do things the next time around.

And So For Parents...

What are the triggers that set you off to loose your self control? Is it being bossed by the boss? Or nagged at home? Or being yelled at by your kids?

How do you make yourself feel better when you are triggered by something? Do you grab a beer or a valium? Tell yourself that you're able to handle the situation?

How do you refocus your energy? Do you try to do something productive? Do you fight back?

Can you and how do you organize your thoughts in the middle of an upsetting experience? Do you problem solve easily or loose the ability to think and have to wait for the intensity of the situation to fade away?

Now that your child is at a stage when his *critical mind* is assisting him in harnessing the powerful energy of his emotions it may be the time to do an overall evaluation of his self-control skills.

We concentrate on the four key areas in this list of statements; the child's ability to inhibit behavior after being triggered, the child's ability to self-soothe, the child's ability to refocus energy and his ability to organize his thinking into a positive plan.

These factors are not presented in order. The questions relate to how the child shows, demonstrates and expresses his self-control abilities in the four domains.

Self-Control Questions

Yes or No answers	Yes	No
1. My child expresses positive emotions easily. 'I am happy."		
2. My child expresses negative emotions easily "I am scared or mad"		
3. My child talks about things that happened in his past		
4. My child talks about things that will happen in the near future		
5. My child asks questions freely		
6. My child usually listens attentively when adults speak		
7. My child usually follows parental directions at home		
8. My child can share toys with others		
9. My child can follow rules when he plays		
10. My child likes to be around his friends		
11. My child can go off for awhile without me		
12. My child finishes most of the things that he starts		
13. My child accepts when he makes mistakes		
14. My child can often calm himself down		
15. My child sometimes takes a leadership role		

	Yes	No
16. My child shows caring feelings for others		
17. My child takes criticism without blowing up		
18. My child seeks help from his parents when he needs it		
19. My child shows some flexibility; he brings up other ways of doing things		
20. My child is good with pets and younger children		
21. My child usually looks alert and happy		
22. My child can try new things		
23. My child looks at people when they talk		
24. My child sleeps alone and eats independently.		

In our rating scale, 20 out of 24 "yes" is *very good*. 15-19 moderate and could use work. Under 10 at this point is a dangerous area.

We recommend going back over the steps and supporting the basics if your child falls into the danger zone. In particular, mirroring, sharing, attachment exercises, and a strong focus on teaching the child to express feelings and to listen to others. Definitely model the 4 areas of self-control for your child. Evaluate your own successes and failures openly and clearly.

It is never too late to make the repairs and at this time in your child's life it is a great deal easier to do now. Take the time to look, listen and feel what your child is saying in all of the ways that he or she expresses himself. The simple fact of focusing on your child might do the trick!

You graduate from this Step with information that will help you teach your child to be a self-aware human being. And this is a critical part of self control and emotional intelligence. Being self-aware means that the youngster will be able to monitor his own emotional and behavioral reactions, make changes and take responsibility for his actions. This, as we know, is an integral part of self control that can only develop when the child is physically and emotionally ready. Now the child is at that stage and you can empower him to be aware of his own behaviors. Although the pathways through later childhood and adolescence present some very formidable obstacles a child with basic self control skills has certain key strengths that help him navigate through the storms.

We look at children with a firm foundation in self-control and we see that they are more comfortable in different situations, they seem to attract other little ones, they listen more attentively and they seem to smile more. These youngsters have a degree of flexibility and resilience when things change and they seek support and guidance while remaining very curious. At times they are impulsive and they stumble and fall and need to practice some basic strategies all over again. That's normal. But these kids seem to want to do better and to be part of the larger social group. They want that shared joy that is part of being a healthy human being even if they have to delay their own gratification. And that is self-control at its best.

When we see a child with poor self- control skills we look very diligently for the bits and pieces that he may well have learned and then we start right there. Many kids have strengths even though they may be hidden and under developed. A child that looks you in the eye for a minute or listens to your voice or lets you touch his hand is a child with promise.

Self- control grows with nurturing, with support and with firm guidance. It must be tended to as carefully as the fragile orchid in the garden or the expensive car in the garage. We recommend that you look for and find the sources of strength in yourselves and in your children and build upon these foundations:

1. Take the time to check your growing child's temperament and see how it changes as he matures. Youngsters will use self control skills to soothe themselves, to delay reacting, to seek new goals and this changes the quality of their temperament. Instead of wailing when they are frustrated, for example you may see the child taking the time to explain what they want.

2. Take a few minutes for face to face interactions and look at your child's expressions.

3. Give a lot of positive feedback whenever your child can delay gratification, or self soothe, or choose an appropriate goal.

4. Review your own self- control strategies from time to time.

Emotional intelligence is the outcome of learning the skills of self control These vital skills become an integral part of the individuals behavior and thinking after years of practice and a great deal of trial and error in the early years. As we now know, there is no perfect E.I.Q and we can only strive for the highest level that is possible for each unique individual.

Part Three: Maintaining Self-Control
Challenge and Self-Control Skills

"It's not over" Marla said to Cathy's mom on the phone one day. Mike shouldn't have pushed Cathy and I talked to him about it. Somehow I thought that he was past that stage already.

"Ha!" Cathy's mom replies. "You're not going to believe this but last week Cathy wanted to sleep in our bed again. We saw a scary TV show and she couldn't go to sleep alone. Nothing worked and believe me we tried everything to make her feel secure."

"I know" Marla sighs. "It's an every day thing, I guess. These kids get bigger and their problems change every minute. I get a handle on one thing and then something else comes up. I have to say though; Mike seems to remember the basic stuff. He knows we love him and he tries hard to be good. Mostly he is good, I guess. It's just so hard sometimes to be a parent."

"That's why boarding schools were invented." Cathy's Mom is laughing at the idea. When they get to be teenagers we will have to consider that as a plan."

It may seem like "Back to the Future" at times when your youngsters face new problems and the old solutions have been packed away in the attic. It may be more practical to keep them handy because these kids will benefit from going back over earlier steps from time to time. And you will have to get creative and think up new ways to help them handle to emotion-loaded situations at school and home and with peers. The challenges and opportunities are, for the most part, brain stimulating experiences.

Way before your children reach their teenage years they will be trying to cope with huge changes in their bodies, traumas around them, the different pressures that adults put on them, etc. etc. To be really honest, break downs in self- control can be expected at any time given the nature of human beings. Even the "perfect" kids loose it from time to time and the "not so perfect kids" face some hard challenges when they have poor self- control skills.

Another dramatic case can illustrate this.

Mark is 10 years old and has been a "stellar child". He had all the usual ups and downs but learned to manage his emotions for the most part and never got into trouble in school. In fact his grades are excellent and he was considering being a doctor just like his Dad until everything went down the drain.

After 20 years of what looked like a good marriage, his parents announced to both their kids (Mark has a 19 year old sister) that they are getting divorced. "We stayed together for you kids." Dad said on the day that he moved out.

Mark was shocked but he kept quiet on that day and for the next several weeks. Later on his father said "I thought that he was old enough to handle that stuff. He's not a baby anymore. Anyway I was sending money all the time."

His mother reported that she was very busy during that time trying to figure things out and get back on track with life. Mark's sister was away in college at the time but later was stunned by what happened with her brother.

Only his closest friends knew that something had changed with Mark and these old friends were cast aside one after another as Mark struggled with the terrible loss, the unexpected, devastating change in his life.

Problems surfaced in school because Mark was drifting away from classes. He was cutting school to be with a new group of kids who somehow related to his "bad attitude". He himself wasn't sure why these school drop-outs and the drug using kids had a way of making him feel somehow better. He couldn't stand being in school with people who were going on with their lives when his was falling apart. He didn't want to be at home in the empty house while his Mom looked for work or hung out with her divorced friends. His Dad called on the phone regularly sounding like he was happier than before. Mark wondered angrily, why he had hated being at home with the family. Obviously, the family and Mark himself counted for very little. What a fool he had been to think that his Dad was interested in Mark's own happiness and progress in school. He felt like the stupidest person on earth. And the most alone.

Nothing that he used to do gave him the same pleasure. He wanted to be back to where he was before but it was impossible. He tried some drugs and drank the beer and for a few hours the world was calm again.

Mark thought that his mother might know that he was using drugs but she didn't bring up the topic. Afterwards she said. "I didn't want him to think that I was spying on him. He was such a good boy.   I hoped that time and his own inner strengths would heal his wounds."

When he was asked about his near fatal overdose Mark said that he didn't know if it was a suicide attempt or just a "cry for help." His parents expressed guilt and sadness about missing the signs that he was falling apart. And yet they are not alone in terms of parents who really believe that strong kids stay strong no matter what. There are so many parents who think that their youngster's capacity for self control will not need their vigilant attention throughout the coming years.

It is an interesting fact, as we think about the maturing brain, that brain development continues into on past the age of 3 and into adolescence. Vital changes occur in areas of the brain concerned with the "higher" levels of cognitive function. What this means is that memory, attention and problem solving skills are still in states of maturation when the child is 3 and 4 and 11 and 12. Their continued self-control abilities depend upon development of these cognitive functions as they grow older. One interesting example is that after age 5 the child can begin to "read between the lines" in terms of statements made by others. In itself this means that they can analyze the meaning of a phrase and not jump to conclusions. The word "jump" is important here because this ability clearly enhances their self control skills. Did you know that children at age 6 are developing the ability to sustain attention? We thought that they could do this already, right? And another example; only after most kids reach <u>age 8</u> or thereabouts can they understand that people get satisfaction from doing what they feel is the right thing. What a concept! It adds to their ability to focus away from the heat of a situation and do what they think is the right thing to do.

O.K., so your 3 or 4 year old is still a work in progress!

So how do parents stay tuned into their kids in ways that help them maintain and increase the strength of their self control systems?

1.   It is useful to keep an *Advanced Temperament Chart*: Your youngster probably looks sounds and feels different when he is happy, angry, scared or depressed. He doesn't express these emotions like a baby anymore hopefully. Take a look at your child in all of his or her moods and write down their individual face, voice and body language ways of showing these emotions.

2. Do a Situational Check: The situation in the home, the school, the family and the community are probably not the same as when your child was a baby. These differences do have an impact. Changes can trigger emotions and emotions can get overwhelming. Take a look at all facets of the child's environment and see what has changed (re-locating, divorce, births, deaths, etc.) and how much it has changed. Here is an example from our work:

> **John is 6 years old. He is a kid with average intelligence and usually does average work in school. Lately he has not wanted to be involved in school activities and his teacher thinks he is "going through some emotional problems." There have been a few small changes in the family situation. Nothing critical, just the fact that grandmother is living with them now because she is lonely and needs some help. John loves his grandmother. Her presence has allowed his mother to spend more time with her own**

**career. After all he's not a baby and grand-
mother can do many of the things that she
used to do.**

**There is one very simple and little routine
that John misses terribly. He used to have
time with his mother after school and he
loved to watch her getting things ready for
dinner. He could chat with her about anything and nothing. John demonstrated his
joy verbally and behaviorally by swinging
his legs back and forth in a happy rhythm.
His cheeks were rosy and his eyes bright.
It was a good relaxed time for him and it
made going to school and then coming
home a pleasant experience. Something to
look forward to. Grandmother is fine but
she sits in the living room and asks him
questions that he doesn't feel like answer-
ing.**

This change is hard for him although it's not a crisis. John
can't find the words to tell Mom how he feels. He's unhappy
and feels let down. At home, if his mother took a temperament
check she would find that he's not relaxed, his face is sad
looking, he doesn't chatter with her when she does come
home. Small changes can be powerfully challenging for some
kids.

3. *Do a Self-Check:* As a parent you are still the key
person in your child's life. Have you changed? Adults do go
through many changes that are reflected in their moods, their
behaviors and so forth. A simple matter of changing jobs can
and does mean that the strengths of the families self control
skills may be tested. Do you come home from work later
now because your children are a bit older? Are you more

tired or impatient? Are financial woes sapping your energy now that the child needs so many more things?

4.   Listen to the opinions of teachers, family and neighbors: Sometimes, other people will see things that you don't or don't want to admit. It can be embarrassing to hear the neighbor tell you about what she saw your precious youngster doing in her backyard with another kid. It can be frustrating to listen to the teacher say that your child blurts out impulsively in class. It can be maddening when your mother in law simply has to tell you what she thinks of your little one. But we, as parents, have to be strong and consider what is being said. Better to hear it now than later on.

5.   Stay positively involved with the youngster: This is often challenging for parents to do as the child becomes more peer oriented and independent. It is important to keep your relationship strong and protective without hindering the youngster's exploratory curiosity. Some pointers are and we call this the "K" list.

> a) Know who your child's friends are by asking questions and making your home as available as possible for get-togethers.
>
> b) Know who your friend's parents are by asking your child.
>
> c) Keep the internet protected from unsafe sites (see resources for young children's internet sites)
>
> d) Keep modeling positive self-control strategies when new situations come up with the child
>
> e) Keep doing fun things as a family no matter how tiny the family is.

It is always possible to do repair work in the domain of self-control when there has been a big or small failure of that system.

Consider Mark's case, for example. It took enormous effort on his part, his parent's part and the therapist's part but the repairs were made.

In his case they started from *Step 2* in re-establishing the trust and security that he once felt with his parents. It may seem strange, but it is true that his parents had to get to know him in all of his moods again. Mark had to get to know his parent's as well.

They eventually found each others comfort zones and the triggers that would cause a loss of control

The family had to re-learn how to read and understand each other's emotional expressions, how to share feelings and let each other go and do their own thing. Mark had to learn that his father's leaving was not abandonment and that his father would respond to his cries for help or guidance. And then they had to practice and evaluate their successes and failures.

In many cases it is possible and it is very useful to start from the beginning of the process of developing self control skills. The early Steps are all about trust, being safe and secure in the hands of those you love, learning to express feelings, and share emotions. The later steps are simply the growth of abilities to be independent and yet close to people and to feel similar feelings so that you can act and react appropriately.

The health of every family and every relationship is based upon the ability of its members to maintain an emotional balance and behave in ways that positively effect the rest of the group. When we look at self-control strategies we can sometimes find entire families who have developed amazing ways to manage unexpected and challenging events.

Some families manage to stick together but have very unhealthy ways of dealing with emotional situations. These families teach unhealthy self control techniques to their children. The result is not as dramatic as in Mark's case. It is however, painful for the kids and the family as a whole and it is quite a common pattern. It even has a name. It is called *The Anxious Family*. Therefore we thought you might benefit from this example.

Tom and Sally have been married for 10 years and they have an 8 year old boy, Adam. They were both born in Armenia and had tough lives until they came to the US. The parents were concerned because Adam's teacher wrote that he was very "anxious" in school and he has no friends and doesn't engage in any sports.

Tom and Sally have struggled hard to come to this country and when they openly talk about their experiences they say that they are often afraid that something bad may happen. Their fears are, of course, closely related to what they have endured and their fragile sense of stability in the new country. They seem to be overly self-controlled people, afraid of saying the "wrong" word or doing something that would call attention to them. All of this is understandable given their background.

What happens in their routine discussions with Adam about school or other subjects is that they tend to do several things:

1. The point out potential dangers in situations

2. They tend to encourage him to anticipate negative responses

3. They express doubt about his ability to handle situations

They do this in very gentle ways, of course, but the effect upon Adam over time is to make him **so** aware of possible triggers and problems and so focused on the inhibiting aspect of self control that he *avoids* everything.

Avoidance is the key word here because we already know that self- control is not about avoiding challenges. A family's anxious pattern of relating and their over controlled style can lead to other problems as well. It can result in the youngster being depressed, or even aggressively acting out at some point.

We bring this up because anxiety is a growing problem and some families and parents think that it is a "normal" part of living in this fast-moving, unpredictable world.

When we move farther along the anxiety spectrum we are in fear territory. Being fearful is also not a healthy part of self-control. Being scared does push some children into silence, and they shut down. It launches other kids into violence, and addiction and various other pathological states. None of these states have anything to do with healthy self control although some adults use fear to get their children to comply.

In our *next chapter* we deal with some of the tough issues that parents may be faced with; violence, shame pathology and the continuity of unhealthy behavior. We talk about them only as they relate to self control and with the hope that looking at these issues will encourage parents to do any work on the Steps that they need to do.

Tough Issues and Self-Control - Shame, Anxiety and Violence

Stories about kids loosing all self-control are very frightening. The media is full of these reports and they trigger our own fear and anxiety and depression. Somehow it is so difficult to conceive of a child pulling a trigger, wielding a knife, hanging himself. And many of us ask ourselves; who was at the controls managing this kid's roller coaster emotions? Who taught him how *not* to react immediately, how to comfort himself and figure out a better plan? The numbers of girls who loose control is mounting. Where are the parents, the relatives, the friends when this girl is cutting deep grooves into her arms, or starving herself, or running away from home?

In a very real way many of these problems have roots in the very early development of self- control. We can assume that there were many missed steps and too few efforts or attempts for whatever reason, to repair the problem.

This is not all about blame. This is all about information that parents need to have at their disposal. And therefore we tackle several areas that are of great importance for your information.

Shame and Self-Control

Ahmed is a 35 year old accountant with a wife and two children. He works hard and he is very conscious of how others rate his work in his competitive business. Ahmed's boss has had to make some serious changes in structuring the firm given the economies sluggishness. All employees are on heightened alert in case downsizing becomes an option. Ahmed is always a bit on edge, lately doing more work and doing it faster. This morning his boss calls him into the office. The man looks upset and several other advisors are seated in the office. The boss's mouth is drawn into a thin line. Ahmed's stomach contracts. Then his boss holds up a folder.

"This is not correct, Mr. Artanian. The numbers have to be wrong. I don't like the work. It's sloppy and not your usual style."

Ahmed can feel his face burn. His throat feels tight and he struggles for the words that he needs to say. Before he can get anything out his boss, shakes his head in disapproval and gestures Ahmed to the door.

He stands outside for a moment feeling himself perspire, almost sick to his stomach with embarrassment. "Why did the boss have to humiliate me in front of other people?" He asks himself. The redness slowly drains from his face as he walks back to his desk. For the rest of the day he can't concentrate. He is sure that everyone around him knows what happened. He keeps his head down when he leaves the office.

The ability to make someone feel this kind of emotion is a powerful thing. Anyone who can provoke this physical and emotional distress in another human being is really in control of the situation. The feeling of shame and its strong physical components makes most people want to do something to feel better. The pain of shame sets many people off on a roller coaster of emotions. One has to have good self-control skills to manage this one. Sometimes adults do have the capacity to hold back, self-soothe, refocus and think constructively when they are bombarded with shame-pain stimuli. ***Children are pretty defenseless against it.***

People use shame-pain stimuli to exert control. Ahmed's boss used it to get him to re-do something, comply with something. Parents also use shame-pain stimuli to get cooperation and compliance from their children. And it is so effective that some parents don't know when to stop pushing those buttons.

Experiencing shame can propel a person to (a) run and hide, (b) confront the person who inflicted the shame or (c) convince the person to change something. In the realm of young children the result is often (a) followed by (b) and rarely (c).

Shame, we know now, when it is used over and over again leads to severe emotional problems including social phobia, panic attacks and sometimes to violence. The pathways from shame to chronic psychological illness and violence have been found.

A case from our practice may illustrate this problem.

Mary is 6 years old and deathly afraid of meeting people. She rather stay alone in her room than go outside or to parties. Mary's parents have always believed that little girls should be clean and neat at all times. Mary has an older brother who used to use her as a kind of target for mud balls, magic markers and other games. He began doing this as soon as she could toddle around. Her mother's response to her was usually; "Oh look how ugly and dirty you are. Not like a proper little girl at all. That's very bad, Mary go clean up. When your father gets home I will scrub you hard in the bathroom." This happened over and over again as Mary tried to stay away from her brother and anyone else who could get her dirty and make her ugly and bad. She blushes easily when called upon in school and she feels ugly because of the red color in her cheeks. It's a never ending cycle of pain for her. Whatever she touches seems to get her dirty.

This kind of crippling cycle is a result of repeated shame experiences in which the child has no way to even begin to self-soothe, to get into a comfort zone. Her only recourse is to hide and berate herself. Shame used in this way does not produce healthy self-control skills. Unfortunately the more attached and dependent the child is on the parent, the more pain he feels when he is shamed.

How do parents usually use shame to control their children and make them unable to use their own self- control skills?

Telling a small child that they are bad, dirty, ugly or stupid. Showing a child he is bad by abusing or neglecting him.

There are also instances in which shame leads to aggressive behavior. Children, teens and adults can explode when they are constantly humiliated and simply cannot control their feelings. The ashamed child is a time-bomb when he or she continues to be bullied in school. They can only run and hide for so long.

Anxiety and Self-Control

Speaking about running and hiding brings us to the role of anxiety in the self-control system. Anxiety, as we know, is part of the fear spectrum of emotions. When we are faced with something threatening we have fear or anxiety depending upon how great the threat is. When a child experiences anxiety or fear and is unable to cope with it, this can trigger a number of responses. The child may try to avoid the triggering person or situation, the child can lash out at the person, the child may panic and be paralyzed with fear.

Fear and anxiety are powerful emotions for little kids to manage.

Threatening a child so that they will comply is not a way to ensure the healthy development of self control skills. What it does do, is get what looks like temporary cooperation from the youngster who then learns to avoid, lash out or become rigid in defense of this terribly unpleasant emotion. After all, a child can't remain in a fearful state for too long. They have to get back to some kind of a comfort zone. Don't we all?

Violence and Self-Control

In one of many recent experiments it was found that spontaneous, impulsive violence is related to failures in the self-control process. It would seem that aggression of any kind is a failure of the whole self-control system but it isn't. In instances of war, and planned murder or retaliation, the self-control system is not where the failure is.

The pathways to impulsive, spontaneous violence are rooted in the person's inability to suppress internal negative emotions (anger, fear) when they are presented with for example, *facial expressions* that are angry and fearful. The "normal" response and one that we have talked about is for these facial signals to inform the person that something needs to be understood. This leads, in healthy self-control to a delay in behavior and then into the strategies we have discussed. The unhealthy response is for the person who is presented with angry and fearful expressions to become overwhelmed with inner anger or anxiety and explode.

Research is still going on in terms of precisely mapping out the pathways to impulsive, spontaneous violence. Early infant and childhood experiences are on the **hot** list of factors that are involved in the failure of adaptive self control strategies.

As the research goes on we hope that parents will not wait to use the data that we already have. Reading the emotional expressions in faces is a vital step in the overall process of achieving emotional health. It is a foundation of self control and the two domains are clearly one and the same.

For many of us it is still difficult to comprehend just how impulsive emotional and physical outburst somehow help the person get comfortable. There are three basic explanations for how it may work:

1. The person lets out or **vents** the emotional energy and this reduces the pain.

2. The person can **avoid or escape** the task or the person that triggered the roller coaster.

3. The person gets **attention** in whatever form it comes and this satisfies some need.

Now that we have some idea of how impulsive aggression may relieve the pain we know that as parents we have to teach the healthy strategies for self-control:

> **Delay,**
> **Self-Soothe,**
> **Refocus**
> **Organize thinking.**

Alternative Teachers of Self-Control

There are numerous instances in which a parent or parents are not the best teachers of self-control skills. Some youngsters are able to learn what they need to learn from people who are consistently around them. This works best if the individual who is teaching the child is not undermined by the parent.

We know about grand-parents, older siblings and teachers who have stepped up to the plate and found ways to teach self-control strategies. These individuals moderate or buffer the impact of inadequate parenting. The key is in the child's receptiveness and the parent's willingness to let it happen.

Parental Perceptions

In many experimental tests with mothers and infants there is some real concern about how the individual perceives his or her child. Sometimes parents read things into the child's behavior or miss behaviors completely. It has been noted, for example that depressed mothers can rate their infants as unloving or difficult to manage. Anxious parents may see their children as too fearless and then try to protect them.

We know that the parent's perception of the child is a key factor in the process of developing self- control skills. While objectivity is very hard to maintain we hope that the knowledge that, as a parent, your view might not be perfect will help you to see things more openly and clearly.

The Behavioral Approach to Teaching Self Control Skills

In this book we use a behavioral approach to the teaching and the learning of self-control skills. The behavioral aspects can be found in our focus on; educating parents, practicing exercises and self-monitoring exercises.

The behavioral approach is usually an active, problem-focused, goal-oriented method. In many cases it works faster than such methods as psycho-therapy and it is also an alternative, in some cases, for medication.

In the realm of working with infants and with children and their parents the behavioral approach is widely used to treat a variety of disorders. One example is of its use with traumatized young children. Even very young kids can be taught behavioral strategies to help them manage the roller coaster of feelings associated with natural disasters, death and molestation. Kids can learn, for example how to do deep-breathing exercises and simple progressive relaxation exercises. The physical nature of these tasks is great for kids who are very physical little beings.

Children learn how to use these strategies when confronted with a strong emotional stimulus. Then they can delay responding, self soothe, refocus and organize their thinking. They control the rollercoaster rather than the roller coaster controlling them.

The great debate over what kinds of treatment to offer kids and when to do it is an on-going thing. It is, however, universally accepted that the earlier they learn about themselves and the world the better off they will be.

What kids learn about self-control will guide them through some pretty difficult times.

Predictions

When your child is very young, say 2 or 3 years old you think that he will change enormously. And your child *will* grow bigger, stronger, more masculine or feminine etc

In truth, some of your child's basic characteristics will endure and remain quite stable over time. This is scientific fact and the most enduring traits are right in the area that we are talking about. *The domain of self-control.*

Young children who have trouble dealing with the roller coaster of their emotions from a young age will probably have similar problems throughout their lives. Not all of these problems are *severe* and in fact adults have all kinds of trouble with self-control issues. But study after study is pointing to the fact that impulsivity, lack of empathy, and other important characteristics have continuity over time. If, as a parent, you see these traits in a child of 3 or 4, you may well see them in various forms when he is 13 and 23.

The kids who have the hardest time are those who struggle along without any help or any repair work from concerned adults. These are the kids whose self control problems make them "different" in school and often rejected by peers. This is where it hurts the most. Youngsters who are rejected *because* they have not been helped to accurately read and understand face and voice expressions, *because* they can't share and follow the rules and *because* they don't seem to remember what happened the last time they got into trouble.

These kinds of problems lead to depression, anger, drug abuse gang affiliation and all kinds of unhealthy strategies. After all, these kids are just trying to feel better. They just need to get off that miserable roller coaster. And they don't know how to get comfortable anymore.

And so we are back to the critical issue of comfort. The emotional ups and downs that make life what it is are wonderful and yet they need to be under some control. Where that comfort zone is and how to get there and then use your brain is the life lesson that we all need to learn, re-learn and practice.

Divergent Pathways and Plasticity

The road map of the human brain is complex and far from complete. Often you start with one set of genes and tendencies and then wind up with a human being who is far different from what anyone would have predicted. This is one reason why we tell parents to "expect the unexpected" and to give parenting 100% of your effort with some healthy open-mindedness thrown in.

Here's one example of how things can turn out OK when you wouldn't expect them to. Some children who have very depressed parents turn out depressed, anxious, avoidant and angry. But others come through it with an amazing ability to empathize with others. Somewhere along the line, during childhood, this skill was developed and nurtured. It can lead to a high degree of emotional intelligence.

The brain is, as we know fairly malleable, especially so in the early childhood years. Child experts count on this ability of the brain to heal, to change and to survive. Parents should also be aware that this is a very real and positive thing. It makes child-raising the most challenging thing you will ever do.

Triple "A" Parenting:
Awake, Alert, Aware

Now that you know all about self-control let's go back and revisit a few places. One of the most important and wonderful things that parents can do is to look for the small but powerful milestones in their child's emotional development. It is true that many of us easily recognize the bad stuff; the tantrums, constant crying, sleep problems, and language delays. Volumes have been written on these issues. The positive stuff is sometimes more difficult to capture. It may be as fleeting as the glow in a baby's eyes or the little finger pointing to something just out of reach. Is it that we consider the positive things to be "normal" and then **expect** it to show up during our child's development?

The tiny but incredibly powerful capacities that lead up to self-control are the most vital parts of our children's overall development in the domain of emotional intelligence. These are the capacities that we have to teach, reinforce and can never ignore. In order to teach it we have to see and understand what it means.

The milestone abilities of face-reading, expressing negative emotions, sharing and empathy seem to pale in comparison to sitting up, first word, walking etc. And yet, these milestones underlie all of the other abilities. Without the ability to control fluctuating emotions what goals can your child accomplish?

Triple A parenting is about finding the small and beautiful expressions that your infant and your child shows you. We mean the wonderful look on your child's face, the tone of his skin, the sound of his voice and his body movements when your child is actively watching you with curiosity. This is the "face" that parents are waiting for; the face of **awake, alert, awareness** that signals parents that his brain is in one of it's best learning modes. This is the face we hope to make parents very aware of so that they can use it for teaching and learning and enjoyment.

Children and adults who are awake, alert and aware are often perceived as smart, well adjusted and great to be with kinds of people. In fact they can maintain good self control over periods of time and this is the **face of emotional health.**

As we move towards a better understanding of emotional health and self-control we as adults can see the benefits of taking care of our own health needs. Sometimes it's easier to do when the benefits are for our kids as well as us. And bottom line is that we are the teachers and teachers who practice their own lessons are the greatest learning models of all. The expression on your face, the tone of your voice, and your body language will convey as much as your words do. Especially to a small child who really doesn't understand all that much about words until later on.

The healthier you are inside, the more you will be able to present the face of emotional health to your child so that your child will learn what it feels like to be an awake, alert and an aware participant in this challenging world.

Part Four: Resource Section

Teaching Tips For Parents

1. Have clear idea about what you want the child to learn. Age appropriate material is important.
2. Chunk the information into bite sized pieces
3. Increase the child's attention to the lesson; you can do this verbally; "This is what we are going to try and do."
4. Have a routine time for teaching and learning experiences
5. Catch your child in his comfort zone and avoid arguments
6. Know your child's learning style; is he an active, hands-on learner or a passive learner who sits and listens and follows directions.
7. Take small steps with frequent rewards
8. Use your face, voice and body language to add positive emotional significance to the lesson.
9. Practice the lesson in play and games.
10. See if the child can apply his learning to a new situation
11. Expect the unexpected with small children and don't feel hurt.

Attention Grabbers

1. The smiling, enthusiastic face and voice go a long way; parent is enthusiastic!
2. Special and favorite place to do the activity
3. Child and parent in relaxed, happy mood
4. Use materials that the child finds exciting to demonstrate a point
5. Use humor; a funny poem or short story before you begin.

Memory Boosters

1. Routine time and place for the activity
2. Use play, stories to rehearse and to remind child about the lesson after it is done.
3. Parents keep a log for themselves of what the goal of the lesson is.
4. End the activity on a positive, enthusiastic note.
5. Relate the lesson to something during the day.

Internet Resources: Parent Information and Kid's Safe Sites

1. The Children's Internet; this is the highly recommended safe kid's site with the most powerful security level possible. This site has dynamic educational material for youngsters of all ages. www.thechildrensinternet.com or www.childrensinternet.com.

2. Zero to Three website; parent information www.zerotothree.org

3. National Attention Deficit Disorder Assn. www.add.org

4. National Assoc. of Cognitive-Behavioral Therapists. www.nacbt.org

5. National Assoc. of Social Workers. www.naswdc.org

6. Learning Disabilities Assoc. www.ldanatl.org

7. Autism Soc. Of America. www.autism-society.org

8. Online Psych: Children's Issues. www.onlinepsych.com

9. Maternal and Child Health Bureau www.mchb.hrsa.gov

10. ChildPsychiatry.Net www.childpsychiatry.net

11. National Institute of Mental Health www.nimh.nih.gov

Counseling and Information Resources- phone

1. **National Alcohol and Drug Abuse Hotline. 1-800-252-6465**
2. **National Council of Alcoholism/ Drug Dependency. 1-800-622-2255**
3. **American Humane Assoc. (child info) 1-800-227-4645**
4. **Access For Infants/Mothers. (AIM) 1-800-433-2611**
5. **Center for Mental Health Services. 1-800-789-2647**
6. **Child Help USA Hotline. 1-800-422-4453**
7. **Depression Awareness. 1-800-944-4773**
8. **Depression After Delivery. same as above**
9. **For Kid's Sake. 1-800-898-4543**
10. **Lamaze International. 1-800-368-4404**
11. **Nat'l Health Info Center. 1-800-336-4797**
12. **National Parenting Instit. 1-909-694-8910**
13. **Parent Help U.S.A. 1-949-251-9274**
14. **Starlight Children's Foundation. 1-800-950-9474**

Other Resources

For Books on Parenting, Child Development and Self-Help see our reverence section. Self-Help books may also be found at www.selfhelpbooks.com

Literature Survey - Books

Brazelton. T. Berry. Neonatal Behavioral Assessment. 3rd Edition. Cambridge University Press. 1995.

Lewis, Melvin ed. Child and Adolescent Psychiatry; A comprehensive Textbook 1996. Yale Child Study Center, Yale School of Medicine, New Haven, Connecticut

Rourke, Byron Learning Disabilities and Psychosocial Functioning a Neuropsychological Perspective 1991 The Guilford Press. New York NY

Braswell, Lauren Cognitive-Behavioral Therapy with ADHD Children Child, Family and School Interventions. 1991 The Guilford Press New York NY.

Flavell, Johnn H. The Developmental Psychology of Jean Piaget 1963 D. Van Nostrand Co. Inc.

Ellison, James and Weinstein, Cheryl eds. The Psychotherapists Guide to Neuropsychiatry; Diagnostic and Treatment Issues. 1994. American Psychiatric Press, Inc. Washington DC.

Goleman, Daniel. Emotional Intelligence. Bantam Books. 1995.

Lonsdale, Loya ed. Guide to Child and Adolescent Therapy. 1996. Hatherleigh Press. New York NY

Sohlberg, M and Mateer, C. Introduction To Cognitive Rehabilitation; Theory and Practice. 1989. The Guilford Press New York NY.

Schore, Allan N Affect Regulation and the Origin of the Self. The Neurobiology of Emotional Development. 1994 Lawrence Erlbaum Associates. Hillsdale NJ.

Pechura, C and Martin, Joseph, Eds. Mapping The Brain. Integrating Enabling Technologies into Neuroscience Research. 1991. National Academy Press Washington DC.

Noback, Charles The Human Nervous System. Fourth Edition. 1991 Lea and Febinger . New York NY.

Begleiter, H and Kissin, B. Eds. The Genetics of Alcoholism. 1995 Oxford University Press .

Fosha, Diana. The Transforming Power of Affect. 2000. Basic Books.

Valenstein, Elliot. Blaming the Brain. 1998. The Free Press. New York NY

Major References Articles

(For convenience note journal name prior to checking with your local library or on-line)

The Prenatal Alcohol Studies

Mental Health Journal; Prenatal alcohol exposure and infant negative affect as precursors of depressive features in children. M.J. O'Connor. Vol 27, Issue 3, 2001 pgs. 291-299.

Infant Mental Health Journal; *Lessons learned from study of the developmental impact of parental alcohol use.* M..J. O'Connor and Olson. Vol 22. Issue 3, 2001 pgs 271-290

Drug Studies

J. of Pediatrics; *Intrauterine Growth of Full-Term Infants; Impact of Prenatal Cocaine Exposure.* Bandstra et al Vol. 108 No.6 Dec. 2001 pgs 1309-1319.

Smoking study

J. Am. Acad. Child Adolesc. Psychiatry; *Behavioral and Neural Consequences of Prenatal Exposure to Nicotine.* Ernst et. al 40:6, June 2001 pgs. 630-639.

Other Studies

Health Psychol.;*The Impact of Prenatal Maternal Stress and Optimistic Disposition on Birth Outcomes in Medically High-risk Women.* Lobel et al. Vol. 19 2000 pgs. 544-553.

Health Psychol. *Life Event Stress and the Association With spontaneous Abortion in Gravid Women at an Urban Emergency* Room Boyles et al. .2000;19:510-514

J of Abnormal Child Psychology. *Nausea During Pregnancy: Relation to Early* Childhood *Temperament and Behavior Problems at Twelve Years.* Martin et al. Vol. 27 No. 4 1999. Pgs 323-

J of Pediatrics. Mater*nal Postpartum behaviors and mother-infant relationship during the first year of life.* Britton et. al. June 2001. pgs. 905-909.

CNS Spectrum. *Brain Hemispheric Organization, Anxiety and Psychosis.* Mucci et al. Vol. 5. No.9 Sept. 2000. Pg.59.

Psychiatric Times. *Brain Development, Attachment and Impact on Psychic Vulnerability.* D. Lott. Vol. XV Issue 5. May 1998.

J. Neurology. *The evocative nature of emotional content for sensory and motor systems.* Loring et al. Vol. 56. 2001 146-147

Infant Mental Health Journal. *Effects of a Secure Attachment Relationship on Right Brain Development, Affect Regulation And Infant Mental Health.* Alan Schore. Vol. 22 No66. 2001 pg. 33.

Infant Mental Health Journal. *Temperament and behavioral problems among infants in alcoholic families.* Edwards et al. Vol. 22 Issue 3, 2001 pgs 374-392

Infant Mental Health Journal; *Depressed mother's assessments of their neonate's behaviors.* Hart et al. Vol. 20 Issue 2 1999 pgs 200-210.

Infant Mental Health Journal; *Mother and infant involvement states and maternal depression.* Rosenblum et al. Vol. 18. Issue 4, 1997. Pgs 350-363.

J of Abnormal Child Psychology; *Parental Anxiety Disorders, Child Anxiety Disorders.* McClure et al. Vol. 29. No 1 2001 pgs 1-10.

American J. Obstetrics and Gyn. *Continuing regular exercise during pregnancy: Effect of exercise volume on fetoplacental growth.* Clapp, James et. al Vol. 186. 2002

Psychiatric Times; *Cognative Neuroscience Encounters Psychotherapy.* Daniel Siegel. Vol. X111 Issue 3. March 1996

Infant Mental Health Journal. *Failure to Thrive is associated with disorganized infant-mother attachment.* Vol. 21. Issue 6, 2000 pgs 428-442.
Beatrice Beebe PhD.

J. Am. ACAD. Child Adolesc. *Psychiatry. Adapting Positive Reinforcement Systems to Suit Child Temperament.* Manasses and Young. 40:5, May 2001.

J. Obstet. and Gyn. *A Randomized Controlled Trial of Intervention in Fear of Childbirth.* Saisto, T et al. Vol. 98. 2001.

Pediatrics. *Extraordinary Changes in Behavior in an Infant After a Brief Separation.* By M. Stein and J.Call April 2001 Vol. 107 No. 4 pgs.822-826.

J. of Abnormal Child Psychology. *A Longitudinal Study of Mother's Overreactive Discipline and Toddler's Externalizing Behavior.* Leary et al. Vol. 27. No 5. 1999 pgs 331-

CNS Spectrum. *Shame and Psychopathology.* Pallanti et al. Vol. 5 no. 8 August 2000, pgs 28-42.

The ADHD Articles

J of Abnormal Child Psychology. *The ADHD Response-Inhibition Deficit as Measured by the Stop Task*. Nigg. Vol. 27. No 5 October 1999. Pp393.

Ibid. *Inhibition and Attention Deficit Hyperactivity Disorder*. Quay. Vol. 25. No1. 1997. Pp7-13.

American Academy of Pediatrics Annual Meeting. *Attention Deficit Hyperactivity Disorder: Current Diagnosis and Treatment*. By Wolraich MD. October 2000.

J of Abnormal Child Psychology. *Confirmation of an Inhibitory Control Deficit in Attention-Deficit/Hyperactivity Disorder*. Schachar et al. Vol. 28. No. 3 June 2000.

J of Consulting and Clinical Psychology. *Self-Regulation of Affect in Attention Deficit-Hyperactivity Disorder (ADHD) and Non-ADHD Boys: Differences in Empathic Responding*. Braaten. Vol. 68. No 2, 2000. pp. 313-321

American Academy of Pediatrics Policy Statement; RE9911 Aug 1999.

Clinical Psychiatry News. *Behavioral Strategies Soothe Traumatized Children*. Bates, Jan 1999. Pg 32

CBS Healthwatch by Medscape. *Children Need Special Attention in Disasters*. By P. Eastman. 9-17-2001

National Mental Health Association. *Helping Children Handle Disaster-Related* Anxiety. Medscape News. Sept 13 2001.

J of Consulting and Clinical Psychology. *Predicting Conduct Problems: Can High-Risk Children Be Identified in Kindergarten and Grade 1?* Bennett et al. Vol. 67. No4, pgs 470-480. 1999.

Journal of Abnormal Child Psychology. *Early Developmental Precursurs of Externalizing Behavior in Middle Childhood and Adolescence.* Olson et al. Vol. 28. No2. 2000, pp. 119-133.

Arch. Gen. Psychiatry. *Parental and Early Childhood Predictors of Persistent Physical Aggression in Boys From Kindergarten to High School.* Nagin et al. Vol. 58 April 2001 pp389-392.

J of Abnormal Child Psychology. *Evidence for the Continuity of Early Problem Behaviors: Application of a Developmental Model.* Keenan et al Vol. 26 No6 1998. pp. 441-454.

Journal of Abnormal Child Psychology. *The Efficacy of Toddler-Parent Psychotherapy for Fostering cognitive Development in Offspring of Depressed Mothers.* Cicchieet et al. Vol. 28. No2, 2000. Pp. 135-148.

Ibid. *Multimethod Psychoeducational Intervention For Preschool Children with Disruptive Behavior; Two-Year Post Treatment Follow-up.* Shelton et al. Vol. 28. N0.3 June 2000.

Journal of Child Psychology. *Treatment of Young Children's Bedtime Refusal and Nighttime Wakings.* Reid et al. Vol. 27. No1 1999. Pp 5-16

Pediatrics. *Baby-Friendly Hospital Initiative Improves Breastfeeding Initiation Rates in a US Hospital* Setting, Phillips et al. Vol. 108. No 3 Sept. 2001.

J. AM ACAD. Child Adolesc. Psychiatry. *Adapting Positive Reinforcement Systems to Suit Child Temperament.* Manassis et al.. Vol. 40. No 5 May 2001 pp 603-605

J of Abnormal Child Psychology. *Behavioral and Emotional Problems in Young Preschoolers: Cross Cultural Testing of the*

Validity of the Child Behavior Checklist ages 2/3. Koot et al. Vol. 25. No3. 1997. pp. 183-196.

Archives of Disease in Childhood. *Quantitative growth and development of the human brain.* Dobbing et al Vol. 48. April 1973. Pp. 757-

Neuroscience and Biobehavioral Reviews. *The adolescent brain and age-related behavioral manifestations.* Spear. Vol. 24. 2000. 417-463.

Printed in the United States
83144LV00007B/156/A